the knot

GUIDE FOR THE GROOM

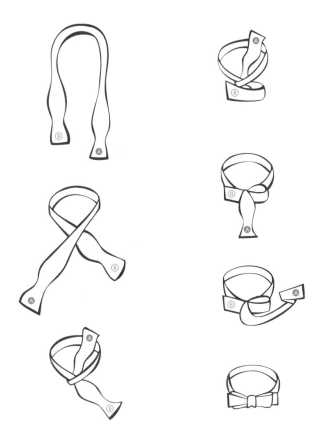

the knot

GUIDE FOR THE GROOM

by Carley Roney

Illustrations by Cindy Luu

CHRONICLE BOOKS

SAN FRANCISCO

Library of Congress Cataloging-in-Publication Data:

Roney, Carley.
  The Knot guide for the groom / By Carley Roney ; illustrations by Cindy Luu.
    p. cm.
  1. Weddings–Planning. I. Title: Guide for the groom. II. Knot (Firm) III. Title.
  HQ745.R649 2005
  395.2'2–dc22
                                2004030995

ISBN 0-8118-4614-8

Manufactured in China.

Designed by Aufuldish & Warinner

Distributed in Canada by Raincoast Books
9050 Shaughnessy Street
Vancouver, British Columbia V6P 6E5

10 9 8 7 6 5 4 3 2 1

Chronicle Books LLC
85 Second Street
San Francisco, California 94105

www.chroniclebooks.com

ACKNOWLEDGMENTS

→→

I am extremely fortunate to work with such a talented and dedicated staff at The Knot. Thank you to all who contributed, from checking our formalwear facts to adding an artful turn of phrase—and a special thanks to Kathleen Murray and Rosie Amodio . . . and to both of their fiancés, who were probably more involved in this project than they bargained for.

This book would not be possible without the insight of thousands of couples who log on to The Knot Web site every day and share their questions, anxieties, and great ideas. Thanks to the brides who dished about what they had (or wished they had) their fiancés handle, and thanks to the willing grooms who shared their own brand of wedding advice with us.

More special thanks: To Victoria Colby, for her creative direction. To Alonna Friedman, for her great research and clever writing. To the team at Chronicle—especially our editor, Mikyla Bruder, for her direction, patience, and clear vision. To Cindy Luu, for her brilliant illustrations. To Jennifer Unter, for crossing all the Ts. To Lisa Campbell, for her painstaking help in putting all the pieces together. And to Rob Fassino, for getting us into the groom business in the first place.

Finally, thanks and love to Havana, Cairo, my dad (the best public speaker I know), and the grooviest groom of all, David.

CONTENTS

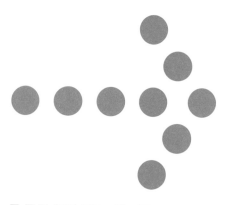

INTRODUCTION

The chances you are simply dying to read this book? Slim. The chances it is going to save you stress, time, money, and embarrassment as you plan your wedding over the next several months? Let's just say it's a lock.

We've always considered it our job at The Knot to keep an eye out for our guy friends. We know you haven't been dreaming about weddings all your lives. That said, since you were lucky enough to fall head over heels—and happen to live in the twenty-first century—you now have a job to do, a wedding to plan. And we are going to help you do it with ease, style, and your manhood intact.

Consider this book your cheat sheet. It's a step-by-step manual for making a wedding happen. Now, we don't expect you to read it cover to cover. Just dip in when you want the facts on what's important to you (or what your bride has decided should be important to you). Here's a quick guide to what is covered where:

Chapter 1

First important detail: decide what type of wedding you want. In this chapter, learn how to . . .

- *Figure out the perfect wedding date, where to throw the bash, and how many people you are going to party with.*
- *Break down the budget and understand how much the wedding is going to cost.*
- *Understand the golden rules of the guest list, from how to cut it to whom not to invite.*
- *Determine your wedding-planning role: will you be Supergroom, pitching in without being asked, or relegated to doing menial tasks that your bride throws your way?*

Chapter 2

If you're like most men, your biggest issue may be trying to comprehend how wedding planning has changed your sweetie. In this chapter, learn how to . . .

- *Understand where your bride is coming from (remember, she's planning a once-in-a-lifetime event).*
- *Take active steps to, as we say, get along until you get down the aisle.*
- *Manage the often-treacherous divide between your mom and your honey.*

Chapter 3

Here we get down to the nuts and bolts of wedding planning, arming you with a detailed vendor hit list. In this chapter, learn how to . . .

- *Pick the right wedding pros by asking smart questions.*
- *Avoid common pitfalls.*
- *Negotiate. We've got tried-and-true tactics that will help you seal the deal.*

Chapter 4

You need to know who's who in your wedding party. In this chapter, learn how to . . .

› *Choose your crew.*

› *Share expectations with your best man, groomsmen, and ushers (we've included useful cheat sheets for you to hand out).*

› *Manage unruly groomsmen.*

› *Soothe your bride's fears about every guy's number one priority: the bachelor party.*

Chapter 5

Unless you're a card-carrying member of today's Rat Pack, you'll probably need a primer on penguin suits. In this chapter, learn how to . . .

› *Know what to wear when.*

› *Tell the difference between the various tuxedo and tie styles.*

› *Add flair with accessories.*

› *Find the perfect wedding band: not too much ring, not too much bling.*

Chapter 6

Here, you'll get an outline of the all-important ceremony. In this chapter, learn how to . . .

› *Decide on the type of service you want.*

› *Choose and interview your officiant.*

› *Pick your readings (hint: enlist your readers for help).*

› *Write your own vows. If your lady wants to hear words from your heart on her wedding day, we'll get you through it with our never-fail vow-writing crash course.*

Chapter 7

This all leads up to the big day. From the night-before bash (a.k.a. the rehearsal dinner) to getting ready for the wedding, we keep you on track with a detailed timeline of events. In this chapter, learn how to . . .

› *Get to the church (or synagogue, or city hall, or garden) on time.*

› *Be a good host.*

› *Make sure you and your bride have a ball.*

› *Give the perfect toast. We've got dos, don'ts, and, for when all else fails, speech shortcuts.*

Here's the deal: twenty-first-century grooms are expected to play a role in organizing their wedding festivities. Some willingly take on—and even enjoy—this role. Others need to be dragged into it. This book will work for you either way—and help you win points with your soon-to-be wife! Turn the page and you will be on your way.

1 → GETTING STARTED

MOST men think the hard part is over once they buy the engagement ring. But proposing is just the first in a long line of decisions. Think of the engagement period as a series of 1,001 questions about things you've probably never considered—like whether your friends are groomsman material. While your fiancée might assume she'll need to lead you through most of the wedding details, keep in mind that this is a big day for *both* of you. Follow this guide to impress her with your planning know-how—and to make sure there's a little of you incorporated in all the elements of the day. A wedding is a huge undertaking. The trick to a successful celebration is to do your homework, set your priorities, and get organized.

This first chapter sets up the groundwork for making sure you and your bride agree on the type of wedding you want to have. We'll show you how to figure it out, pick your priorities, and determine your (realistic) wedding-interest level. Being very clear—with yourself and your fiancée—about where you want (and don't want) to be involved is a must. Finally, we'll cover the big prep essentials: figuring out the wedding finances (like who's going to pay and how much things actually cost) and surviving the guest-list debate. Just remember: a wedding education is your best asset for a stress-free engagement period.

THE BIG PICTURE

The first step in crash-course Wedding 101? Deciding on your wedding MO. Before you set a budget, create the guest list, or celebrate at your engagement party, sit down with your fiancée and talk about the exact kind of wedding you want. This decision will set the tone for your entire day—and all the other details will follow suit. Consider the time of year, size of event, and style with which you're most comfortable. And exercise the great art of compromise (your marriage will thank you for it): if you've always envisioned a celebration with fifteen friends on a beach in the Bahamas but your fiancée comes from a massive Irish-Italian family, start thinking *happy medium*.

THE FIRST DATE

Your opening move is to tackle the calendar. Consider seasons that are significant to you. Always loved summers at the shore? Or are Henleys and spiked cider more your thing? Or think about a senti-mental date (parents' anniversary? first time you kissed?) that you'd love to commemorate. Avoid dates that present potential conflicts of interest (special holidays, the big game) and bear in

Seasonal Beverage

mind how long you want the engagement to last. A wedding date less than six months from your proposal will be more stressful, yet there won't be time for fickleness on the part of your fiancée. On the flip side, a long engagement (more than a year and a half) will alleviate some gotta-get-it-done pressure but may allow too much time for scout-ing out the "perfect" vendors.

Option 1: Spring Fling

May and June are always packed with weddings, with good reason: the sun shines longer, flowers are in bloom, and the season itself symbolizes renewal. But spring weather can be unpredictable. If you decide to have an outdoor wedding, an emer-gency rain tent will be essential.

Option 2: Summer Lovin'

With warm temperatures and sublime sunshine, summer guarantees a good time. The cocktails alone—margaritas, mojitos—conjure up a smile. Weddings in these months often tilt toward the slightly less formal, with light suits and plenty of bright colors. But carefree summer-bash fun can dissipate in hotter-than-hot temperatures. Investigate extra air conditioners in case Mother Nature makes a sizzling call. And give guests a heads-up about your wedding date long before their summer vacation plans are set in stone.

Option 3: Fall Ball

Sure, June weddings are always the thing—but other months such as October are clearly in vogue. The changing leaves and crisp autumn air provide perfect wedding scenery, and you don't even have to pay for it! Lots of couples are keen on autumn, so book early.

Option 4: Winter Wonderland

Depending on the region where you hold your wedding, the warmth and intimacy of snowy winter can't be beat. Think fur stoles, overcoats, and hot chocolate with Schnapps. But beware: the benefits of off-season discounts can fizzle quicker than you can say "blizzard" (think: transportation disasters).

→ → → **GAME DAY**

Avid sports fans will want to steer clear of key dates like the World Series, Super Bowl Sunday, and March Madness—especially for three-day-weekend weddings (a growing trend). You won't want guests (or  yourself!) to be preoccupied by the game and spend the whole time searching for the latest score. But if you're the ultimate sports fan and your fiancée's down with it (there's always a chance), incorporate the game into your day with formal pictures at the stadium and tables named for favorite teams.

ON WHOSE TURF?

Choosing a venue is a hefty decision. The place sets the mood for the event and will be where you spend the most dollars and time. First, think big: in which city (or country!) will you do the deed? (We'll delve into specific venue preferences, such as ballroom versus beach, in chapter 3.)

Option 1: Bride's Hometown

Traditionally the bride's family pays for the wedding, so her hometown may be at the top of the list. Consider the pluses and minuses of this situation: Your fiancée's parents know the area very well, which means they'll have plenty to say—and their guest list may triple due to the locale. But her parents might also be a huge help in organizing the affair, taking some strain off you and eliminating an abundance of blind research. Does your fiancée crave the sentimentality of getting married at her childhood home? Then you won't want to disappoint her. An at-home wedding can be especially personal, but with logistics to nail down—like renting portable toilets and hiring a parking valet—there may be additional costs and stress.

Option 2: Groom's Hometown

You might also consider *your* hometown, especially if someone in your family is too ill to travel or you have a summer home just longing to hold a party. Just make sure your parents are comfortable with transforming their home into the wedding's home base.

Option 3: Your Current Hometown

If you both feel that your roots are in the city in which you now live, go for it. It'll be easier to make appointments with vendors and keep tabs on the reception site. However, since you may be entertaining both sets of parents, there could be added tension. And the need for organization will increase, since the number of out-of-town guests will double.

Option 4: Neutral Ground

A new option quickly gaining steam is the destination wedding. Having a wedding far from home used to mean that you were eloping, but now many couples are planning intimate, inclusive celebrations overseas. Why wed away from it all? Destination weddings are relatively low on stress: many resorts and popular vacation spots cover most of the legwork, your guest list practically cuts itself (eliminating potential list-making drama), and you get to spend a few days with your nearest and dearest—instead of just a few moments in the receiving line. Sounds amazing, right? Broach the topic with your fiancée—though her parents may be married to the idea of a wedding in her hometown, she might be up for something more adventurous.

SIZE MATTERS

Ensure an etiquette-friendly engagement by figuring out the size of your wedding (small, medium, or large). This will help shape people's expectations. You won't need to keep the wedding a secret from coworkers if you establish early on that the guest list will be limited. The size will also play a huge factor in your budget. Feeding 400 requires a bigger wallet, obviously, than does wining and dining 60 close friends.

Option 1: Larger than Life

Want to (or have to) invite everyone you've ever met? Then a big wedding (more than 150 guests) is for you—especially if you love a party. When you share your wedding day with more than 200 guests, it's bound to be the social event of the season. You won't have to worry about offending anyone by not inviting them, but you may not get to spend a lot of time with each guest. Basic costs (for meals, reception rentals, and so on) will be significant, and finding a site with charm—as well as a big capacity—may be difficult.

Option 2: A Manageable Medium

Many consider 75 to 150 guests the ideal wedding size. You'll be able to spend some time with everyone, and the numbers won't overwhelm your budget. But going this route will fill the guest list with gray areas. Aside from those you obviously don't have to invite, you'll face an internal struggle over whether to include others—and you may have some explaining to do. The more recent your college graduation, the more difficult this option becomes. Two years out of school, everyone still seems like your best friend. Seven years after graduation, your list changes dramatically. (We'll guide you through guest-list planning strategies on page 32.)

Option 3: Small and Snug

Thinking of an intimate affair (under 75 people)? You'll be sure to have plenty of quality time with all your guests, but get ready to say "We're keeping it small"—to everyone from coworkers to second cousins to long-lost pals from high school—about a zillion times. Draw up your guest list immediately to avoid raising hopes unnecessarily. If you go for quality over quantity, you'll save big bucks—unless you're serving Kobe beef and rapper-worthy bubbly, of course.

After the initial excitement over your oh-so-romantic proposal, someone may want to throw a formal bash for you. Typically held no later than four months after the big announcement, an engagement party is meant to provide an opportunity to share your nuptial news with future wedding guests and begin joining your two families in a festive way.

Your future in-laws are the traditional hosts of this meet and greet, but your parents may offer to plan the party instead. If the wedding will take place in your betrothed's hometown, your parents may feel like doing their part. Close friends of yours (the best man and his significant other, for instance) might also host the party. The hosts are simply whoever feels so inclined.

→ Invite right. Don't include anyone who won't be invited to the wedding, but don't feel pressure to invite everyone on the guest list. The engagement party should be intimate, especially if your two families are meeting for the first time. If her parents have a stronghold on the wedding guest list, your parents may want to host a party to celebrate with their friends (who may or may not be invited to the wedding). This is totally acceptable, as long as everyone is aware that the wedding guest list will be limited.

→ Register early. Presents are optional for this event, but most people will want to bring a gift. It's smart to register early for items in a low price range, say, under $100. Guests will appreciate the gift-giving help, since they'll know they're getting something you really want. But don't offer up this info—that's tacky. Let guests know where you're registered only when asked. (See more registering tips on page 70.)

→ Work the room. Many guests will know only you or your fiancée. Eliminate the great divide by introducing different groups of people to each other. Make an effort to personally greet everyone—and introduce yourself to guests you don't know.

→ Head off embarrassment. Is your mom telling—again—the tale of how you vomited on the bus in second grade? Laugh it off, but then pull her aside and ask her nicely to stop. She may be nervous about meeting this many new people and so is relying on humor as an icebreaker.

→ Return the favor. When well-wishers propose a toast to you, remain seated with your drink in your hand. It's customary for one or both of you to then stand and respond with your own words to toast the host, thank people for coming, and express your excitement about the upcoming occasion. Single out each set of parents and raise a glass acknowledging their love and support. And don't forget to say something nice about your bride and how happy you are to be marrying this incredible woman. It will make her melt—every time.

SUSSING OUT STYLE

You should be able to describe your wedding in three to five words. And, believe us, you'll be asked. Some examples: summer wedding at the shore; black-tie ballroom affair; backyard tent at home; retro glam in a loft space. You get the idea. This thumbnail description will also help you make future decisions about what fits and what doesn't. You and your fiancée should share the same basic wedding vision—you won't want to book a funk band when classic '50s is what she's after. Here's the quick and easy way to determine your wedding design.

Step 1: The Feel Factor

What's the vibe you're looking to create? Fun and festive? Calm and classic? Swanky? Formal? Frat party? Relaxed? Every element must work together to capture the wedding mood—you can't force a black-tie affair into a rustic lodge.

Talk to your fiancée about your gut feelings about the wedding's ambience—your realistic gut feelings.

Step 2: The Look

Believe it or not, color is king at your wedding (you'll probably hear the words "wedding colors" much more often in the coming months than you'd ever think possible). Maybe you don't care about color now, but you may care later when you end up surrounded by yards of pink chiffon. Give some thought to your favorite color. Deep red and chocolate brown say elegant, while purple and chartreuse are totally chic. Then think about what you want to wear and what you envision guests wearing. If tuxedos with tails are your thing, follow suit with an überformal affair. If seersucker suits are more your style, suggest a beach bash. What setting makes you most comfortable? That's where you're guaranteed to have a good time.

A. Classic Ensemble

B. Rock Band

MUSICAL STYLES

When calling up friends and family to share the news, or when socializing at your engagement party, you're bound to be bombarded with the invasive questions nearly every to-be-wed faces. Not to worry—we have some answers:

Q. Who is paying for the wedding?

A. We haven't worked out the details yet.

Q. When will you start having kids?

A. Let us get through the wedding first!

Q. Where will you live?

A. We're still deciding on that, taking one step at a time.

Q. How much did the ring cost?

A. Plenty!

DECIDING ON YOUR ROLE

GROOM GUSTO

Traditionally, the groom is responsible for the band, cars, and honeymoon. But these days, even the manliest man wants (or needs) to have a say in the other details of his wedding day. First, start to figure out what role you want to play in your wedding. Establishing your interest level up front will (hopefully) leave no room for dashed expectations on the part of your fiancée. Ask your bride where she stands on your participation. Will she insist that you help choose all the vendors? Does she truly want to know whether you prefer coral or copper? Or does she want to use you as a well-informed wedding sounding board? Planning success is all about finding that magical point where both you and your fiancée are happy with your participation level. How much groom gusto do you have?

HOW FAR ARE YOU WILLING TO GO?

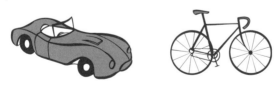

A. The Modern Marrying Man

B. The Guy with Priorities

C. The Silent Partner

THE VIRTUAL GROOM: Hit the Web to set up a wedding Web page. Stop rolling your eyes. Sending guests to your online page will eliminate the need for you to repeatedly explain the details about the wedding location, driving directions, where you're registered, the date and time, and who's in your wedding party. As things develop, you can update your page to keep people in the loop. Include contact information for people to use in case of emergencies (your groomsmen, perhaps?). This can be a fun project for you to helm—especially to ensure a minimal cheese factor.

Role Model #1: The Modern Marrying Man

Interest: High. You really care about making sure the reception site has the right vibe, the chairs are up to snuff, the photographer produces well-designed albums, the band can play your favorite tunes, and the cake has the right mix of flavors. Basically, you want to have a say in most decisions and make sure the wedding is a true reflection of you *and* your fiancée. You're every bride's prince charming.

Time commitment: Huge. You'll be there every step of the way.

How to make it work: Your fiancée probably knows that you care about appearances and the finer points of entertaining, so most likely she's already comfortable with your level of enthusiasm. However, you don't want it to seem like you're stealing the show. Always compliment her wedding-planning prowess first, and then offer your opinion. Make sure you clearly divide and conquer tasks—and don't get too stuck on your own ideas.

Pitfalls: Don't be offended if vendors are surprised by your taking charge. A proactive groom is nothing new, but people may be amazed by your gusto. Don't let the wedding pro think dealing with you is a waste of his or her time—be prepared with smart and direct questions.

Role Model #2: The Guy with Priorities

Interest: Specialized. Calligraphy and aisle runners may seem trivial to you, but there are certain things you'd like to have a say in (or at least veto power over). Think about what you want to remember most about the day: Maybe you're a foodie and want to have full rein with the menu selections. Or perhaps you appreciate fine photography and want to flip through a plethora of portfolios. That's great—you'll have a better chance of attending a party you'll really enjoy, rather than suffering through an expensive tribute to Preston Bailey (Hint: he's a wedding planner extraordinaire).

Time commitment: Average. In the areas you really care about (or that are assigned to you), you'll need to devote a lot of time working out the kinks with each vendor. Also expect to clear all decisions with your fiancée before and after they've been made.

How to make it work: Let your fiancée know which area you really care about and that you want to help make the final decisions. Tell her you'll take care of scoping out possible vendors and setting up appointments for you both. She'll love you for it.

Pitfalls: When it comes to wedding planning, remember that the elements should all work together. Many couples create a unified look by using the same style or colors for the invitations, cake, and flowers. So even though you've made it known that the cake (and just the cake) is your forte, your choice may be dependent on another choice, and another one.

Role Model #3: The Silent Partner

Interest: Limited. Plain and simple: whatever she says goes. It's not that you don't care about your wedding—you just don't know the difference between buttercream frosting and fondant. You leave the design decisions up to her, to whom they really matter. And that's fine. Just be supportive, not dismissive, when asked for your opinion.

Time commitment: Low. She'll drag you along to meet her final vendor picks, she'll constantly show you magazine pictures of things she likes, and she'll expect you to help with any DIY project she's dreamed up (although, depending on difficulty level, this could amp up your time commitment to high).

How to make it work: Put on a good show and act like you want to participate, even if you leave everything up to your fiancée. Develop an opinion on a vendor—any vendor—and stick with it. Indifference just ticks off any bride. Seriously. Know that low involvement equals low veto power. You can always *try* to persuade your fiancée to change the boutonnieres to a more masculine color if you feel threatened by pink.

Pitfalls: Since you don't show a strong interest in any particular wedding-related issue, your fiancée may randomly assign you responsibilities. You must do these tasks, and do them well. If she gives you a task that you really aren't comfortable with, like selecting the ceremony readings, speak up and ask for her help. Always elicit her aid from the start, rather than disappoint with a job not done well.

THE FAMILY MAN

Once you know how involved you want to be with the wedding planning, take it to the top. The groom's family often plays a tricky role in weddings—often a nonexistent one. So while you may not care about the receiving line, your parents may. And as your family's elected rep, standing up for their interests is a must.

Parental Preferences

Before going to bat for your parents' interests, know exactly what they are. At the very least ask them about their priorities. If they are vegetarians who would appreciate more meatless menu options, bring this up with your fiancée. If they are professional swing dancers, try to find a band that can play swing tunes as well as funk and disco tracks. Or they may have total trust in you and be thrilled to simply be a part of the day.

Money Talks

Many times the balance of power tilts toward the bride's side, regardless of who's covering the cost (tradition can be a tough nut to crack). But even if your parents *aren't* contributing, they probably don't want to be dissed and dismissed. Just because they're not paying, will they have no say? Talk to your parents about the natural correlation between investment and involvement (we'll delve deep into how financial participation can change the game later in this chapter). The more money they contribute, the more power you'll have to make their interests known.

Hands-on Help

If your parents want to earn decision-making privileges, suggest that they pitch in with the planning work. But act as liaison between them and your bride to avoid stepping on anyone's toes. If your fiancée throws herself into designing the perfect invitations, don't say that your mom thinks navy-blue ink is better than black. But if she needs help stamping and stuffing, see if your mom (or dad) is willing to commit time to the task and be part of the process.

DOLLARS AND SENSE

For better or for worse, all wedding decisions start and stop at the budget. You can't book a thing until you total all the dollars you have committed–from your families and from your own bank accounts–to this affair and decide how to allocate the funds. With the average price of a wedding roughly equivalent to that of a new car, it's a hefty investment. For some, the cost of a wedding is their annual income; for others it's more, less, or anywhere in between. But don't worry–weddings can be affordable and manageable, no matter what your budget.

BREAKING DOWN THE BUDGET

Reception: 50%

Half of the overall wedding costs will go to food and drink. Figure it this way: The last time you went to a nice restaurant with another couple and ordered cocktails, a bottle of wine, and dinner, what was the cost per person? Now multiply

Budgeting Tools

that amount by your projected number of wedding guests. To-be-married math totals are rough stuff. You can begin to see why reception expenses are so high–it costs a lot to entertain that many friends and relatives. In addition to charging for food and beverages, some sites levy a flat-rate fee just to use the space. Depending on the cachet of the site (museums or art galleries, for instance), these fees can skyrocket.

Attire: 10%

Sorry to say it, but the majority of these funds will go toward your bride's gown. Budgeting for this area really depends on your fiancée's taste–if she won't settle for anything less than designer wear, you can expect a price tag in the mid thousands. If this worries you, suggest sample sales to your bride. We know of one Supergroom, armed with specific gown information, who battled the racks to buy his lady's dress at a fraction of the retail cost. As for your dapper duds, investing in a tuxedo is a very cost-effective idea–especially if you've got a flurry of weddings on the horizon. (See chapter 5 for more on your wedding wear.)

Photo and Video: 10%

This is one of the three vendor biggies, aside from the food and venue costs. Your photographer will most likely spend an average of eight hours shooting the entire day, and the fee is reflective of this dedicated time. Also consider the hours spent processing and editing the film, and meeting with you to go over proofs. Albums are generally an additional cost, so be sure to ask about pricing—especially when the photographer won't be passing along the negatives to you (this means you must order your album through him or her). Videographers can cost just as much as photographers, depending on style and finished product. Raw footage will run much less than a highly edited tape with a highlight reel, a soundtrack, and special effects.

Flowers and Decor: 10%

It may seem shocking, but your florist will probably cost just as much as your photographer. Consider the workload: bouquets, boutonnieres, corsages, ceremony flowers (altar arrangements and/or a chuppah), reception centerpieces, cake topper. And fresh flowers are surprisingly expensive. A single calla lily can cost as much as $15 a stem! Many florists will design the entire space, adding lanterns, plants, and lighting, which can lead to—you guessed it—more money.

Music and Entertainment: 10%

The final vendor category in the high-cost triumvirate is entertainment. And it's worth it: music often makes or breaks a wedding. Top-rated wedding bands usually charge per musician, so if you're pushing your budget to the limit ask if you can hire a nine-piece ensemble instead of the full twelve-piece band. Just be sure you know which musicians are in the truncated group. Disc jockeys, being one or two individuals, can cost significantly less—unless you nab Ibiza's hottest export, of course. Don't forget to ask about music for the cocktail hour, which might not be included in the fee.

Invitations, Rings, Gifts, Etc.: 10%

Other items add up—things like paper products, wedding bands, wedding party gifts, the ceremony site and officiant's fees, transportation, tips, taxes, and other miscellaneous expenditures (like a coat-check person, if necessary). Generally, 1 to 2 percent of your budget is spent on each category, but if you're looking to de-stress your savings, it's better to put your money (and your time) into what you and your bride care about. So if you want to give your groomsmen really nice thank-you presents, consider spending less money on your wedding wheels.

Other Expenses

Wedding Coordinators

If you and your fiancée seek the unbiased help of a professional (often a relationship saver), you'll need to allocate an additional 10 to 15 percent of your total wedding budget. However, many wedding planners offer tiers of services ranging from planning the entire event to simply providing vendor recommendations, causing the overall cost to rise or fall proportionately.

Honeymoon

This is one area where grooms are expected to really step up–and you'll probably want to anyway. Traditionally, your parents pay for the honeymoon but, with post-wedding getaways turning into two- to three-week vacations, you and your fiancée may want to take care of this yourselves. The cost, naturally, will depend on your traveling tastes, but remember to budget for it!

→ → → **YOUR SAVINGS POTENTIAL**

My monthly income
x .20= _____ (A1)

A1 x months of engagement
= _____ (B1)

My honey's monthly income
x .20= _____ (A2)

A2 x months of engagement
= _____ (B2)

B1 + B2 = Total potential wedding budget

PICKING POCKETS

Traditionally, the bride's parents cover the cost of most everything wedding related, leaving his family to take care of the groom's attire, boutonnieres, officiant, grooms-men's gifts, and the bride's wedding band. These days, this rule seems pretty archaic. The bride's parents probably won't be expecting to take out a third mortgage on their house to pay for the wedding, but neither will your parents be expecting to get away with only paying for the rehearsal dinner. Most likely, you and your fiancée will be pay-ing for part (or even all) of the wedding.

Step 1: Calculate Your Own Funds

Figure out how much money you and your fiancée can spend. How much have you saved so far and how much can you ante up if you stick to a rigid savings plan? It's increasingly common for couples to bear the financial burden completely, alleviating family tensions for everyone.

Step 2: Set Up a Sit-Down

Schedule a time to talk to both sets of parents about money matters. It's a good idea to have two separate meetings—you don't want to highlight economic differences and augment awkwardness in what already might be an uncomfortable conversation. Many parents say from the start whether they plan on contributing, but if they don't it's all right for you to broach the subject.

Step 3: Be Frank

Let all parties know that you're beginning to create a budget and are wondering what their plans are. If your future in-laws have already paid for another daughter's wed-ding, they may assume the same rules apply here. Hopefully, they'll come to the table with a specific amount that they're willing to contribute. If not, review your basic budget breakdown and give them a general idea of what you're hoping they can offer. And remember to show your gratitude!

Step 4: Create Your Budget

Once you have everyone's expected contributions, add it all up. Spend wisely!

Here's what to expect from three different payment plans.

Bride's Parents Pay

Discuss with your fiancée what their contribution means. Will they insist on having final decision-making power? Will they see this as their party and not yours? If you honestly feel that the gift may lead to turmoil, consider politely rejecting the offer. Have your fiancée take the lead here. Perhaps suggest that they cover the cost of one or two big-ticket items, like the band or florist. The *only* way to avoid hard feelings will be for everyone to be clear about expectations.

Paying the Bills

Both Sets of Parents Contribute

In a perfect world, both sets of parents would willingly chip in what they can afford and cede control of the purse strings to you and your fiancée. But keep in mind that all contributors may expect to have a big say in the day. Another option is the perfect split, where you and all your parents evenly divvy up the costs. This approach works best when all parties are in a similar economic boat.

You and Your Fiancée Pay

Perhaps you've steadily saved since you first landed a job. If you can swing it, go for it. You'll have wedding-planning autonomy and maybe your parents will respond with a phenomenal wedding present, like a down payment on a new home.

MANAGING YOUR FUNDS

Now that you've come to terms with the likely cost of your wedding and your jaw has returned to its natural position, devise a plan for dealing with the dough. Look at the wedding as a small business venture. There are several ways to control the celebratory capital.

Bank It

Open a bank account devoted specifically to this enterprise so you can track exactly what you spend. When dealing with so many vendors and huge price tags, it can be way too easy to agree to frivolous upgrades without recognizing the economic impact. Bottom line: know your limits. A good way to prevent overextending your wedding allowance is to collect all the contributions before you spend a dime.

Save Face

Decide with your fiancée the amount you'd like to allocate from your respective savings accounts to your new wedding account. Once you've transferred this lump sum, create an additional savings plan. Most to-be-weds break their wedding budget slightly, and some exceed it exorbitantly. Prevent bridal bankruptcy by setting up an automatic monthly transfer from your checking account to the wedding account. Pick a sum you can afford each month to devote to the wedding—a slow but steady way to build up your wedding cash.

Reap the Benefits

Take advantage of the high cost of weddings and sign up for a new credit card with a rewards program. Whether it gives you airline miles, hotel perks, or cash-back incentives, using this reward credit card to pay wedding bills will help you accumulate thousands (and we mean thousands) of rewards points. You might get a major deal on your honeymoon, just for using the card to manage your wedding funds!

Lean on a Loan Shark

No, not really. But some couples do take out loans to help cover the wedding costs. Have big wedding dreams but not enough stashed away to accommodate the budget? This may be a good option. Inquire at your bank for lending options, but be forewarned: typical loan terms apply. You'll have to make at least the minimum payment each month, so don't promise your princess a fairy-tale wedding if you really can't swing it.

Whether you're thousands of dollars over budget or just a couple hundred, here are some savings options perfect for you.

Slash and Burn

1 The only way to save significant wedding dollars is to cut the guest list (remember, half of the budget goes to wining and dining your guests).

2 Ask the site if you can bring in your own wine and liquor. Purchasing in bulk from a discount store can save plenty. Or if you're paying by the number of bottles consumed, consider offering table service rather than open bar access, in order to limit the frequency of refills and floaters.

3 Skip live cocktail-hour music. The cocktail hour is for chatting it up. Trust us, no one will notice if you stream in prerecorded music that you've mixed yourself.

4 Go local. Vendor travel fees can really add up—especially if you're marrying in a high-traffic area or overnight accommodations are required.

5 Eliminate ceremony flowers. Besides the bouquets and boutonnieres, of course. Guests will be so focused on the two of you that they won't even notice the unadorned altar.

6 For the invites, avoid multiple and costly pieces (inner envelope, reception card, direction card). Stick with a beautiful invitation and reply card, and direct guests to your wedding Web site for all other pertinent information.

Trim the Fat

1 Instruct the banquet manager to provide sandwiches or other inexpensive meals to the band and photographer instead of the filet mignon you'll serve to guests. (Check their respective contracts for specific food requirements.)

2 Look into the benefits of registering at certain retailers. Some stores offer a discount on your wedding ring if you register there.

3 Cut down on the number of ushers. Think about it: each groomsman and usher receives a boutonniere and a gift. Having groomsmen act as ushers will put a small dent in your floral bill.

4 Pick one cake flavor. Cake bakers often charge extra for making layers in different flavors.

5 Cut one item from the dinner menu. No one will miss the soup if they're filling up on mini crab cakes.

6 Mix metals. White gold looks very similar to platinum—for less than half the price! Plan to upgrade your wedding bands on your first anniversary.

GUEST LIST GOLDEN RULES

We say it over and over again, but the guest list is the biggest factor in calculating the total cost of your wedding–and it can be tough to decide who makes the cut. No spreadsheet has more power than this one in the wedding world. Your watchwords: *evaluate, negotiate, and compromise.*

THE VIRTUAL GROOM: Hit the Web to manage your guest list. An online guest-list tool will help you track the number of guests in each party (great for calculating the total number of invites necessary), categorize guests into A and B lists, and keep track of RSVPs.

EVALUATE

First decide on a target number determined by the space capacity and what your budget will allow. You can invite approximately 10 percent more guests than this figure, since between 10 and 20 percent of those invited typically decline. Make a list that includes everyone you want to celebrate with. Organizing your family's side of the guest list is your responsibility, so start jotting down names in categories to make sure you're not forgetting anyone: family (cousins, aunts, uncles), friends, coworkers, your parents' friends. No censoring at this point, though it's best to be realistic and create a loose formula for everyone to follow (for example, no kids under fifteen, and no second cousins) to keep future cutting to a minimum. Finally, separate your names into an A list (the must-invites) and a B list (the nonessentials–no, we don't mean people you don't like but rather colleagues you might be able to skip).

NEGOTIATE

Technically, whoever picks up the bulk of the wedding bill has final say over how to split up each side's allotted number of invites. A more egalitarian tactic is for the couple to divide the total number three ways between the two families and themselves. Another option: the couple draws up their own list, which includes essential family members and family friends from both sides, then assigns each set of parents a number they can add to that group.

COMPROMISE

If you've followed these guidelines and you still have 300 names and a location that holds 175, sharpen your compromising skills. While you might feel bad about deleting names from the list, you and your fiancée need to develop guilt-free parameters for cutting. It's not necessary to invite your entire fraternity pledge class if you haven't seen half of them since college. Focus on people who are relevant to your life now, and who will be around five years from now. That couple you keep bailing on dinner plans with? They can probably go to the bottom of the list. The key to the cut is to do it as efficiently and quickly as possible, kind of like removing a Band-Aid—to ease the pain.

→ → → **DO I HAVE TO INVITE . . . ?**

Couples Whose Wedding You Attended

You don't have to invite couples you're not close with anymore just because you went to their weddings. If anyone will understand, it's those who have done this before.

The Office

It's not a bad idea to invite your boss, especially if you plan to stay with your company. Choose the superiors you work with the most—half of the time they'll decline, note your generosity, and just send a gift. As for other coworkers, a good rule of thumb is to invite people you socialize with outside of work. If you invite some coworkers and not others—particularly if it's a small office—ask those invited to keep it on the down low. And prepare for awkwardness, even after the invitations are out and RSVPs are in.

Significant Others

Some friends may try to set up dinner dates with you and your fiancée around the time invitations are going out, in order to ensure their significant other is invited. Their thinking? You'll see them as a couple and feel obligated to invite both. To counter these tactics, set up rules saying who can bring a date. Traditionally, it's couples who are married. But these days, it's often those who live together or are engaged. Whatever the case, create your own guest-list guide. That way there are no hurt feelings when some people get invited solo.

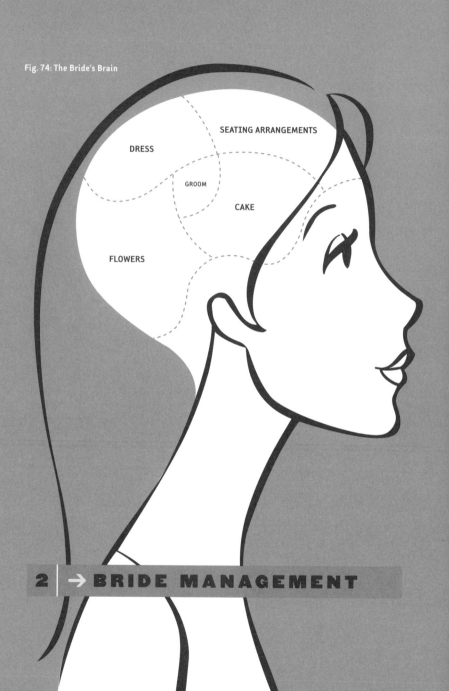

Fig. 74: The Bride's Brain

SEATING ARRANGEMENTS

DRESS

GROOM

CAKE

FLOWERS

2 | → BRIDE MANAGEMENT

SHE seemed sane when she was your girlfriend, and now you barely recognize her? Your betrothed is simply suffering from a case of wedding mania. Don't worry, it happens to the best of brides—and we promise you, it will go away. Instead of feeling held captive by her wedding-induced moods, try to ask her where she's coming from: Is she stressed? Overwhelmed? Scared? In this chapter we'll give you an insider look at her temporary insanity. We'll also give you great ideas on how to make it better, like communicating with one another, and we'll suggest other ways to relieve some planning pressure. Finally, we'll let you know how to manage relations with *your* mom (often a point of stress for brides), so you can minimize tension between her and your fiancée.

GETTING ALONG UNTIL YOU GET DOWN THE AISLE

THE PRESSURE . . . OF A PARTY

Many women are wired for weddings. Chances are, the minute details of the big day are much more important to her than to you (and if not, all the more power to you!). Throwing parties, deciding on a wedding look, picking out a color palette—most women are drawn to the creative expression of entertaining and the esteem of being the perfect hostess. Your bride may not fit into this exact mold but, whatever the case, be prepared for your role as celebration cohost. Find out what's really motivating her and try to make it work for both of you.

Motivation Factor #1: The Need to Impress
The wedding is a very big reflection of who she is, particularly to her girlfriends. And who doesn't want everything to go perfectly when friends are watching? She's craving *oohs* and *ahhs*—she wants people to compare other weddings to hers for years to come.

Smooth groom move: Make her wedding dreams come true. If she desperately wants baby-blue chairs, find a reliable rental company and make the deal. Or come up with a great favor idea that fits perfectly with the wedding theme (scour wedding magazines for ideas or ask married friends for inspiration).

Motivation Factor #2: The Need to Please
She may be feeling pulled in ten different directions, possibly working with opinionated parents and an unopinionated fiancé. It's a classic power struggle that leaves her totally exhausted. Her mom and overzealous sister may each be calling her three times a day to remind her of something she should be doing. The stress can be a lot to bear—and whom will she take it out on? You, naturally—her best friend and confidant.

Smooth groom move: Step in and step up. Make a decision. If everyone is bickering about invitation selections, research the matter (see chapter 3) and pick out a style.

Motivation Factor #3: The Need to Breathe

She, like you, is also dealing with the conflicting emotions surrounding this next phase in her life. She's thrilled with the prospect of being married, but it's a big transition. You, better than anyone, can understand that. So while she's internally reflecting on the fact that you two will be together until you're old and gray, she's outwardly investing those emotions into planning the perfect wedding. Sometimes we just control the things we can.

Smooth groom move: Remind her of why she said yes. Surprise her with a fabulous night on the town—and if she wants to talk wedding, let her.

TALK ISN'T CHEAP

We know you've heard it a thousand times, but who can't use a reminder every now and again? Communication is key. Wedding planning requires a lot of patience on your part and involves a lot of stress on hers. There are certain hot spots that will get her flummoxed, frustrated, or even fed up with the whole thing. All that's needed is a little TLC (totally loving commitment).

Reply Right

Instead of escalating her annoyance by acting, well, annoying, you need to ask her why she's upset and what you can do about it. Sometimes she'll want to bounce ideas off you; other times she'll just want you to "yes" her. The rule of the ring finger: you know your fiancée best. If she's asking for an opinion but you sense she wants reassurance that her favorite is the right choice, agree with her ("Yes, chocolates do make great favors").

Lend an Ear

The best advice is to listen to what she is saying. When she panics about how she doesn't think the wedding will come off, don't throw out a nonchalant "It'll be great." The worst thing you can do is to seem uninterested—indifference is a bride's number one enemy. So listen up and offer a solution. Even minor resolutions to her planning panic attacks will win you major pre-marriage points.

THE VIRTUAL GROOM: Hit the Web to bone up on the etiquette. Wondering what you're supposed to give your bride for a wedding gift? Don't know how to tell your future mother-in-law that your best friend won't shave his mustache? You can find solutions to your etiquette problems straight from the pros.

Support Her

Compliment her often. Tell her how much you appreciate all the time and energy she's investing in your big day, because more than anything she wants you to love the wedding. Remind her of what a caring guy you are and why she fell in love with you in the first place. Maybe she just needs to vent. Encourage her to let it all out—and offer a shoulder to lean on. She may even repay the favor later—in bed.

Shut Up

Even the most rational, logical women occasionally get bent out of shape over the smallest wedding details. Your tactic: To avoid blurting out the first words that come to mind (which would certainly result in a lot of negative repercussions), refrain from speaking for one minute. Once you've stepped back from the situation, you'll understand that she's stressed and needs soft-spoken words of wisdom.

→ → → **SPEECH THERAPY**

Here's how to articulately speak your mind to your stressed-out bride.

→ When you WANT OUT of something: "I'm honored that you trusted me to select a love poem for the ceremony, but it's really your forte and I could use your help."

→ When you WANT IN on something: "I'm so proud of how you're coordinating colors for the wedding party clothes, but I'd like to help you find some other options besides purple polka-dot ties for the groomsmen. Can we do this together?"

→ When you are FRIGHTENED by something: "Wow, the butterfly logo on our invitations is so lifelike it could almost fly off the page, but I'm not that much of a nature buff. Maybe we can find something that reflects our mutual interests?"

→ When you are ANGERED by something: "Thank you. You worked hard to come up with a seating plan for our 500 guests, but the table for my college buddies is so close to the kitchen they might be mistaken for waiters. Let's see if we can put them somewhere else."

→ When you are ADAMANT about something: "I understand how much you love that Michael Bolton song, but our first dance is really important to me too and I'd like to suggest some alternative tunes."

→ When you just want to THROW IN the monogrammed towel: "Yes, dear, I will wear some blush so my pasty skin looks better in the photos."

YOUR UNDECIDED BRIDE

The universal truth is that many brides agonize over details and have a hard time making decisions. Her indecisiveness might clash with your amazing ability to pick and choose with confidence, but for the sake of relationship harmony, you'll need to support her. You *will* be pulled into the discussion, so be prepared with a wedding-friendly answer. As she waffles back and forth, be patient and try to figure out why she's unable to sign off on a certain detail.

Problem: She's obsessing over wedding colors.

Rationale: She wants to make the right statement at the wedding. A detail like color (for the flowers, dresses, linens, invites) contributes to the feeling of the day. She wants everything to fit together.

Solution: Give her the chance to run through the options. When she asks which shade of green best complements the ocean-view ballroom, she's not being funny—at least, not on purpose. If you have an opinion, tell her, or pick a color at random—it just might be the one she's looking for!

Problem: She can't choose her bridesmaids.

Rationale: This is most likely the result of not wanting to hurt anyone's feelings. It may not be such a big deal for your boys to suit up and walk down the aisle, but girls have an emotional investment in their wedding parties. Right now she's evaluating her friends' relative importance, and it makes her feel terrible.

Solution: This is one time where she really doesn't need you to join in with pros and cons about her friends. Instead, suggest she limit the bridal party to just family members. It's an easy out.

Problem: She's not respecting your decisions.

Rationale: She may have the big picture in mind. If you met with a reggae band for the cocktail hour but the wedding mood is black-tie big band, she may think it's not the right fit. Or maybe she just doesn't like your taste.

Solution: Gently call her on it. For instance, if you've already expressed your preference for a certain photographer and she keeps sending you links to new portfolios, don't dismiss them. Ask what it is she doesn't like about the shooter you've picked out. Maybe she's not thrilled with the album options. Regardless of the reason, explain that you're comfortable with this photographer—and that if she can find another with a similar style and more favorable albums, you'll be on board.

To you, changing her name may seem like a no-brainer. It follows years and years of tradition, right? But it's increasingly common—and acceptable—for brides not to change their names. Here's why she might follow that path:

Identity Fraud: Your fiancée may feel that just because she's getting married she shouldn't have to assume a whole new identity. She has lived with her surname her whole life and it's a part of her persona. Lots of guys and gals grow up being called by their last names. How would you like it if suddenly you weren't "Miller" anymore?

Job Security: She may have carved a name for herself at work and changing it professionally could be detrimental to her reputation and confusing to her clients—especially if she's in a field like writing or acting, where established bylines and credits come into play.

Spelling Snafus: She may just dread using your last name. Going from a one-syllable surname to a six-syllable one can be tough for anyone. Or her new monogram might spell out something odd, like "F.A.T." Consider creating a new name together. Combining some letters from her last name with some from yours may be the perfect solution.

Even if she agrees to take your name, she'll need time to adjust. Don't pester her or feel insulted if she doesn't seemed thrilled by the prospect. It's important to respect her decision.

EASY WAYS TO HELP THE BRIDE RELAX

A. Foot Massage   B. Hand Massage   C. Neck Rub

COUPLE KARMA

Your bride shows no signs of bridezilla-like qualities—even once the planning pressure sets in. She constantly amazes you with her cool, collected calmness. You may have something to do with that—your involvement or even slight interest in the wedding has put her at peace. She's not overly stressed, but she does want to savor the excitement of the engagement period. Continue this free-loving flow with even more macho moves.

Tactic #1: Be Proactive

Take a day off from work and devote it to wedding planning or doing whatever she'd like you to do, such as running errands that have dropped to the bottom of her list. Or help motivate her to exercise and blow off wedding-planning steam by offering to work out with her. Join her at the gym or local track. If nothing else, you'll look svelte in your tux.

Tactic #2: Be a Homebody

Order in, set up dinner on the coffee table, and rent a wedding movie. (C'mon, Martin Short is really funny in *Father of the Bride*.) Show her you're going to be the perfect husband by doing the dishes. At the very least, take out the garbage.

Tactic #3: Be an Escape

Institute "W-free Wednesdays," a day of no wedding talk. Or when she's anxious about the wedding, offer up a quick back or scalp massage. It doesn't need to be sensuous, just relaxing.

Tactic #4: Be Her Rock

When she does show subtle signs of frustration, annoyance, or anxiety, lend an ear. Let her vent and bear no judgements—blowing off steam will literally keep your bride cool.

THE VIRTUAL GROOM: Hit the Web to browse for your bride. When she complains about not being able to find some wedding object she's looking for, spend fifteen minutes on the Web the next day and send her a couple of links. Not only will it show you care, but it'll also prove you're actually paying attention to what she says.

Since the thought counts more than the price, you don't need to be extrava-gant–sentimentality goes a lot further. Here are some ideas to make her swoon. Note: You can give this gift to her any time in the days before the wed-ding, perhaps at the rehearsal dinner, or on the morning of your wedding.

→ Jewelry: Classics like diamond studs, pearl drop earrings, or a diamond bracelet are good options that will never go out of style. If it's something you want her to wear on the wedding day, make sure it goes with her gown–but don't be offended if she decides not to flaunt it.

→ A scrapbook of her life starting from her bare-bottomed baby days and extending to the present, when she's still a babe.

→ Some sexy lingerie or a dress for her to wear on the honeymoon.

→ An iPod filled with her favorite songs–including your first-dance song.

→ That vintage handbag she's been eyeing on eBay.

→ A bottle of her signature perfume.

→ A book of love poems with a sappy inscription from you.

→ A framed piece of original art to dress up your new home. (Make sure this is art she'll love.)

→ Antique lace hankies (ideally with her new initials on them, if she's taking your name).

→ A romantic love letter or flowers on the morning of the wedding.

BRACELETS FOR YOUR BRIDE

A. Vintage Look   B. Modern Style   C. Classic Design

FOSTERING THE FAMILY TREE

If you and your bride come from similar backgrounds, yours may seem like a modern-day arranged marriage. Be thankful. Remember, when you marry your fiancée, you're marrying her family too! But even when it appears that your families are two peas in a pod, the reality is that every family has its own culture, with weird quirks and tradi-tions. And if the two of you were raised with conflicting religious beliefs, different economic statuses, and individual style preferences, it's important to be cognizant of this so you can create a well-oiled joining-families strategy.

Present a United Front
If you don't already know her family, suggest a get-together. Be prepared for scrutiny, but be yourself—the self with good manners, engaging conversation skills, and respect for his elders. Even if you've felt like part of her family for years, make sure you and your bride act like a team and establish that all wedding decisions will be made by you two.

Understand the Situation
You know how your family works. Share your family secrets with your fiancée. If your mom likes to hear herself talk a lot, let your fiancée know so she doesn't get annoyed with Mom's suggestions. If your dad seems quiet, explain that he's not upset—that's just how he is. Ask the same of her so you can comprehend the roles *her* family members play.

Compromise Styles
Try to find that elusive happy medium where both families' tastes are represented (or at least the more acceptable ones are!). Is one side not comfortable with a superluxe five-course affair? Consider toning down the day's formality with a black-tie-optional buffet. Combine religious traditions. Serve filet mignon and Guinness on tap.

Manage Your Mom
Understand that there might be some tension between the two ladies in your life, your mom and your fiancée. Nobody says you have to choose between them but, unless you want your dream girl to turn into a complete nightmare, you should be a good son and an even better husband. No matter what, side with your bride. Be prepared to stand up to your mom and call her out (nicely) when she's acting unreasonably with your fiancée.

On the other hand, you may not see it. And you may not find it odd that your mom still buys you underwear or always wants to know your whereabouts. But when your fiancée mentions it, don't dismiss her concerns. No one wants to marry a mama's boy—sorry to say it. Try to see things from your lady's point of view: she's up against your mother, who doesn't want to lose hold of her son, which can be a pretty tough place for any woman. Your best bet: Draw up territory lines. Only broach big discussions with your mom once you and your fiancée have made a united decision. On the flip side, don't let your fiancée criticize the way your mom dresses.

If your mom feels left out, ask your bride to include her in one wedding-related outing or call her to talk about a recent style decision she's made. Take them both out for a relaxed lunch or coffee where no wedding talk is allowed. And, in the end, invest in caller ID.

→ → → **CAN YOU SURVIVE YOUR BRIDE?**

Take this quiz to find out.

1 She asks what you think of the flowers. You think they're ugly. What do you say?
a. "They're gorgeous. I love them."
b. "They're disgusting—what were you thinking?"
c. "I love the color."

2 She asks you to look at a photographer's portfolio. How do you respond?
a. "Yeah, right. I'd rather pluck out all my nose hair."
b. "Sure, but let's work out a good time for both of us."
c. "Just choose one of the twenty we've looked at."

3 She says you both need to write your own vows. Nothing could make you more nervous than public speaking. How do you tell her?
a. "In that case, the wedding is off."
b. "I was thinking of miming my vows."
c. "I'm kind of scared. Can we find a way to compromise?"

4 She's on a kick to take ballroom dance lessons, but you have no desire to go all Fred and Ginger on your guests. How do you let her down?
a. "Hear that crack? I just broke my leg."
b. "I hope the instructor is hot."
c. "If you want to learn a new dance, let's go for something with a little zing to it, like the tango."

5 She's chosen fuchsia dresses for her bridesmaids—and that means your men will be wearing ties to match. How do you change her mind?
a. "If the guys stick with black ties, you and your girls will stand out more."
b. "Your maids will look like big, bright pigs. Oink!"
c. "I will never allow my groomsmen to look all '*Queer Eye*.'"

6 She's looking into a honeymoon in Bora-Bora, but the budget calls for something closer to home. What do you say?
a. "I hate foreigners."
b. "The beach is a great idea, but we'd spend more time on the sand if we flew somewhere closer."
c. "I already booked the Super 8."

1 **The correct answer is C.** Focus on an aspect you like, to show that you are listening. Don't lie by saying you think the flowers are gorgeous. She'll see right through you and pursue a fight about how you always "yes" her. Count on nothing. Be ready for anything.

2 **The correct answer is B.** Agree to the task but make sure she doesn't dictate where and when. Don't harp on the fact that you think she's interviewed too many photographers. Wedding photography is a costly endeavor, and you won't want someone annoying following you all day. You need to be at this meeting!

3 **The correct answer is C.** Don't make a joke. She takes your vows very seriously. If you are truly against writing your vows, tell her—and you'd better have a reason other than you're embarrassed. Reassure her that you love her but that you'd prefer an intimate exchange of words right after the ceremony—alone. Maybe the two of you can meet in the middle: write vows together that you can both repeat, instead of each presenting your own original monologue.

4 **The correct answer is C.** You need to think quickly on your two left feet. This answer shows you're not shelving her idea, just offering an alternative. She thinks a fancy dance routine will heighten the day's drama. Going for something more unusual, like a mambo, will let her have her drama but keep it light so you don't feel like a klutz. Or you might both decide to pass on the performance and instead make a stellar entrance by Rollerblading into the ballroom!

5 **The correct answer is A.** No need for a porcine comment, although we hear ya. Anything that plays up the importance of her posse is a good tactic. Let them have the spotlight while you and the A-Team lay low. High-five her for coming to a decision, then ask for input on the men's formalwear—bow ties or straight ties? She'll be thrilled that you want in on the planning. You're working together!

6 **The correct answer is B.** She has big dreams; you want big-time action. Don't piss her off. Share in the fantasy for a few minutes, and then bring her back down to earth. Present ideas for a destination with a similar feel but a much different (read: cheaper) price tag. In the end, what she really wants is to be alone with you somewhere far from the wedding hubbub. It won't be hard to sway her.

3 → A GUY'S GUIDE TO WEDDING PLANNING

E-mails from old friends who expect invitations

Guest list

Unsolicited advice from Aunt Susie

Ideas you can't afford

EVEN if you don't care what flowers grace the reception-site restrooms, you'll need to understand what wedding planning's all about—after all, this is what will be consuming your fiancée, your parents, and therefore, you too for the next several months. In this chapter we break it down for you, nice and simple. Start with a timeline of tasks, so you won't think it's crazy when your gal starts shopping for a gown with ten months to go! We'll also give you the goods on finding vendors, some negotiating tricks (there's always room), and the nitty-gritty on contracts. No extraneous info here: we focus on what you—the groom—really need to know about picking the wedding pros. If you're using all the relationship savers we gave you in chapter 2, and you can make it through these next twenty-four pages, your woman will be teeming with delight.

TO-BE-WED TIMELINE

Wedding planning works like a game of hoops. It starts off with major action—lots of points in the first half (translation: all you two can think about is the wedding). The third quarter winds down and seems to drag (translation: you don't have much to do). Suddenly the fourth quarter hits, and your team goes on the offensive before time runs out (translation: you're scrambling to deal with and confirm all the last-minute arrangements). Now, here's your game plan. (Note: We assume you have a year to deal. If you have more than a year, there'll be more time to plan and/or discuss; less, and you'll need to tackle a lot at once.)

Twelve (or more) months before:
- ❏ Decide on a budget.
- ❏ Start guest list.
- ❏ Finalize date and time.
- ❏ Scout ceremony and reception sites.
- ❏ Reserve officiants.
- ❏ Choose wedding party.
- ❏ Research vendors.
- ❏ Decide whether to hire a wedding planner.

Eight to ten months before:
- ❏ Register for gifts.
- ❏ Enjoy your engagement party.
- ❏ Book ceremony and reception sites.
- ❏ Book caterer.
- ❏ Book reception music.
- ❏ Book florist.
- ❏ Book photographer.
- ❏ Book videographer.
- ❏ Meet with your officiant to discuss ceremony requirements.

- ❏ Research wedding insurance.
- ❏ Finalize (read: fight about) guest list.
- ❏ She shops for her gown.

Six to eight months before:
- ❏ Block hotel rooms for out-of-town guests.
- ❏ Send save-the-dates.
- ❏ Finalize your registry.
- ❏ Book ceremony musicians.
- ❏ Book a cake baker.
- ❏ Start planning honeymoon (finally, something fun!).
- ❏ Start planning rehearsal dinner.
- ❏ Order your invitations.
- ❏ She orders bridesmaid dresses.

Four to six months before:
- ❏ Book a rehearsal-dinner spot.
- ❏ Finalize menu.
- ❏ Book hotel room for wedding night.
- ❏ Select wedding rings.
- ❏ Decide on groomsmen's attire (never underestimate how important nice tuxes are for pictures).
- ❏ Reserve rental equipment.
- ❏ Book your honeymoon.
- ❏ Plan a stress-free weekend away to remember why you're getting married in the first place.

Three months before:
- ❏ Choose your music selections.
- ❏ Order wedding cake.
- ❏ Order rings.
- ❏ Give groomsmen formalwear information.
- ❏ Chime in on the bachelor party.
- ❏ Hire wedding-day transportation.
- ❏ Shop for a gift for your bride.

Two months before:

- ❑ Mail invitations.
- ❑ Write your vows.
- ❑ Get anything you need for international honeymoon (such as passport, visas, and vaccinations).
- ❑ Purchase gifts for wedding party.
- ❑ Decide on ceremony readings.
- ❑ Send out wedding bands for engraving.
- ❑ Buy any accessories you need (such as cuff links, shirt stays, and a pocket square).
- ❑ She books a makeup artist and hair stylist.
- ❑ Remember to tell your fiancée how much you love her.

One month before:

- ❑ Apply for marriage license (yep, you're really going through with this!).
- ❑ Attend your bachelor party.
- ❑ Buy gifts for your best man, groomsmen, and ushers.
- ❑ Send rehearsal-dinner invitations.
- ❑ Decide on song lists for the ceremony and reception.
- ❑ Create wedding programs for guests.
- ❑ It only gets busier from here—dress and tux fittings, seating charts, delivering welcome baskets, writing checks for outstanding balances, and on and on. (See page 124 for a detailed day-of checklist.)

WEDDING GODS, TAKE IT AWAY

The to-be-wed timeline is pretty intense–that's why a wedding planner can be a busy couple's best friend.

WHO THEY ARE

As the name implies, a wedding planner is a for-hire professional consultant who knows everything about, well, planning a wedding. How do you decide if you need one? Wedding planners aren't just for the rich and famous–pulling off a wedding is a major production. If free time isn't on your side, hiring a planner may be in order. If the wedding is out of town, having a local contact can make it easier on everyone. The one saving grace for your budget is that many consultants have tiers of services from which you can choose.

WHAT THEY DO

The most expensive planners are hired on a start-to-finish basis. They know the best vendors and how to cut deals with them, and they do all the legwork, saving you a lot of stress. All you need to worry about is showing up and making the final decisions. If you can't afford a full-time coordinator, there are ways to use her services without burning a hole in your pocket. Most can be hired on a per-project basis. Call one in when you need somebody to scout locations or to offer advice on trustworthy vendors. It's also possible to retain a planner to oversee the details on the evening before and the actual day of the wedding. If your bride and her mom have been handling every detail, we strongly encourage them to get a day-of planner. If someone else is in charge, any last-minute messes will get taken care of at the wedding–and your bride won't have to blink.

ENLISTING THE EXPERTS

Half the battle of planning is finding the right pros—ones who exhibit solid work, good recommendations, an understanding of your personal style, professionalism, and a personality that's compatible with both of yours. But if you take our step-by-step approach, you'll get everything done, and done well.

Step 1: Do Your Homework
Employ a dual strategy for collecting recommendations by both going online and asking friends. Message boards are a great way to find vendor rants and raves from like-minded couples. If someone can't stop spouting praise for their band, shouldn't you check out the group? Once you've settled on a reception venue (we'll dig into those details on page 55), ask the catering manager or on-site coordinator for suggestions. These folks witness countless weddings every year and know who's good.

Step 2: Check Them Out
Next, make appointments with potential picks in each category. Go slow. Reviewing five photography portfolios in one day is crazy. Instead, consider mixing up vendor meetings each day, seeing one or two photographers and a wedding band in one afternoon, for example. Arm yourself with pertinent questions for each vendor (see samples later in this chapter). Make sure one of you brings a notebook to jot down basics (ask for price estimates as well as other logistics, such as the number of band members and their travel requirements) and write up your initial impressions.

Step 3: Make a Decision
Once you've reviewed potential candidates and their estimates, made sure the price is right and that your personalities mesh, call references. You'll work with each vendor for months to finalize contracts and review plans, so you want to be sure they do what's promised. Ask if they've done something similar to what you're looking for. You don't want your wedding to be a test of anyone's creative capabilities.

Step 4: Make a Deal
Once you've got your man or woman, seal the deal. Even if you're working with the hottest vendor in town, there's always room to negotiate, especially if there's a good

reason for reduced costs–like having the wedding on a less-popular Friday night. While steep discounts are unrealistic, there's a good chance at getting extras (an additional hour for your reception, a champagne upgrade, or an assistant) thrown in. You just have to negotiate right. (See below for tips.)

→ → → **THE NITTY-GRITTY ON NEGOTIATING**

Vendors will bargain with you only if they like you. No one wants to give a jerk a deal. Here are other crucial pointers.

Know the market. Find out what other vendors offer for the same price point, and use this as leverage. Ask about every single thing that's included in your package. Then find out in advance what extras are going to cost–and whether those costs can be waived.

Stick to your limit. A vendor may be willing to cut you a deal as long as you agree to something additional–for example, he might consent to give you an extra hour of shooting, but only if you have him take your engagement photos. What you need to ask yourself is whether this will actually cost you more in the end.

Adopt a friendly but firm demeanor. There's no harm in politely asking for a deal. If vendors are excited to work with you, they may be more willing to come up with creative solutions.

But be indifferent. You need the vendor to believe that if he or she won't meet your offer you will walk away. Consider collaborating with your fiancée to employ the old good cop-bad cop routine.

Practice makes perfect. Try your hand negotiating at a flea market to see what talking style works for you.

Step 5: Sign on the Dotted Line

Once you've talked your way into a deal that suits everyone, get it in writing. Don't settle on anything with just a handshake–and don't assume anything is free. Make sure your contract lists all details, like dates and times, and specify exactly what you will get and when. (See page 54 for a detailed hit list.) Get ready to put down a deposit, usually 10 percent but possibly up to 50 percent. Balances are typically due on or immediately before the big day.

All contracts should be highly detailed and include the following:

→ Business name, address, and phone number

→ Contact person

→ Person responsible for your event

→ Date of the wedding

→ Complete description of product or service, down to the minutiae (for instance, it shouldn't read "band" but rather "sixteen-piece band, including one drummer, two saxophonists, one guitarist, one bassist, and one singer")

→ Length of service (exact start and finish times, including setup and break-down)

→ Hourly overtime rate (make sure your vendor will be available for overtime)

→ Exact prices, including tax, service tip if required, delivery fees, and payment schedule

→ A staff dress code that's appropriate for your wedding

→ Cancellation/refund policy

→ Person responsible for picking up equipment after the wedding

THE BIG DECISIONS

Some choices will define the look and feel of the wedding—these also tend to be the biggest-ticket items. Your fiancée will expect you to weigh in on these make-or-break wedding decisions: venue, food, entertainment, and photographer. Here we've broken down each vendor type with points to remember, insider tips to ensure that you get the most for your money, and pitfalls to be aware of. No one's going to make a monkey out of this groom!

VENUE

Location, location, location. No decision is more important when it comes to weddings (besides whether to have one) than the venue—it sets the mood for the day and provides the style foundation for all other decisions.

Your options:

Ballroom or hotel. These classic nuptial settings, perfect for formal events from strictly traditional to over-the-top glam, see lots of weddings so there's usually good in-house help (before and during the wedding). Since these types of sites tend to be more restrictive (possibly limiting the decorations you can use or forcing you to use in-house services, like catering, for example), these aren't for you if you want to hand tailor every last little detail and can't be flexible about it.

An art museum or historic home. These special sites can provide unique ambiance, whether old-world elegance or modern pop-chic, that's truly priceless—but they're generally rented by the hour (read: $$$$). You may be limited in what you can do decorwise, and it's unlikely that the party can rage all night long. But how cool to marry in a local landmark!

A private home. Particularly if it's a place where the bride or groom spent time growing up, a private home can be an especially intimate and personal place to host a wedding. Remember, there are many more details to consider, from setting up the caterers' prep area to figuring out how to keep guests from tramping through the whole house.

The great outdoors. Few event designers can compare with Mother Nature, whether you wed on a scenic stretch of coastline or in a wooded glade. But you're outside—and that means taking on more site-specific issues than usual. Rain? Mud? Mosquitoes? You'd better have a plan.

Key points: There is often a site fee for certain venues (private clubs, loft spaces), which typically depends on a location's popularity for hosting weddings. Whatever you decide, you need to book the venue pronto. Dates and times are limited (Saturday nights go first, especially in May, June, September, and October) and you'll want to snag a slot before another couple steals it. Take into account how many people the room (or beach or barn) can hold, and then consider how many people you want to invite. Figure out what's more important—the setting or the guest list.

Inquiring minds want to know: How many hours will you have the site? Can you bring in your own liquor? Does the venue have enough electrical power to support the sound system or any lighting you want to add? Where does the band usually set up? Is there a smoking area? What's the staff-guest ratio? You get the idea.

Watch for: A disgruntled site manager. He or she will be the gateway for all your vendors, so you especially want to make sure he or she is professional, pleasant, and accommodating. You may have to visit the chosen venue several times before the big day and familiarize all your other vendors with the space. The site manager should make this happen smoothly.

FOOD

There are two things most people remember about weddings: the music (which we'll talk about next) and the meal. The meal is also what makes up the bulk of the reception fee, since dinner prices are quoted per head. Many locations have preferred or in-house caterers. If your site doesn't require you to use a particular caterer, you will need to choose one for his quality—food you'll enjoy eating too—and together work out a way to feast in style and on budget.

Your options: There are lots of ways to serve a meal: sit-down, buffet style, or passed hot and cold appetizers. A sit-down dinner, with an average of five courses, is elegant and classy but often the most expensive dining option. A buffet gives guests an array of choices, from a raw bar and carving station to a sushi bar and pasta station—and it's probably going to cost less than serving a multicourse meal.

Key points: That ancient castle wasn't built with a microwave. If you're marrying in an unusual setting, make sure there are kitchen facilities. If not, ask your caterer to calculate the cost of renting a mobile kitchen or opt for food that can be served at room temp, such as poached fish. Likewise, if you want your favorite restaurant to cater the affair, make sure they have the ability to serve two hundred people—at once. Go with the catering service that can guarantee high-quality food to a crowd. Above all, avoid grumpy (read: hungry) guests by serving a mix of hearty and light hors d'oeuvres before the meal.

Inquiring minds want to know: Will the caterer arrange for a tasting before booking? Are they willing to include favorite recipes or menu suggestions? Are linens, tables, chairs, and dinnerware included in the fee? Is the caterer working other weddings on the same weekend? Do they charge corkage fees? Are you allowed to purchase a set amount of liquor yourself? Are kegs allowed? (Note: Kegs are far more economical than bottles, and your boys will probably appreciate your devotion to draught.)

Watch for: Service fees. Make sure a fixed gratuity and employees' fees are included in your total bill. Service is a huge (we repeat, *huge*) expense—and you don't want to be surprised by extra labor costs.

ENTERTAINMENT

A bride and groom put a lot of faith in their wedding musicians: it's really the band or DJ's role to make sure everyone—and we mean everyone—has a really good time. Start your search early, since many bands get booked well in advance, especially if they're known to keep people of all generations on their feet all night long. Ask for a video promo or a CD sampler so you can get a feel for their sound, but keep in mind there's nothing like the energy of live music.

Your options: The ultimate wedding conundrum: band or DJ? Let's start with the band. The type of musicians you hire will set the tone for the reception. Depending on your tastes, you might hire an eight-piece ensemble or a full-blown funk band complete with oversized horn section. Just be sure they can play your favorite songs and won't be opposed to you and your buddies stepping in to jam on a song or two—if that's your thing.

If you go the DJ route, check out his collection (Black Sabbath or Sinatra?) and personality (mellow or flashy?). A DJ is usually less expensive than a band, but some people (mainly your parents) may think it's not appropriate for a formal affair. We say, if you'd rather have a person spinning your favorite songs so you can hear 'em the way they were recorded, a DJ is an obvious choice.

Can't find anything that thrills you but won't offend your parents? The cocktail hour is a great place to add personality. Consider hiring a steel-drum band or a mariachi band, or even an old-time banjo crew. Sometimes your reception band will provide musicians for the ceremony and/or the cocktail hour for a small fee. (Remember to ask if they're trained in the type of music you want.)

Key points: Make sure the bandleader or DJ is aware of your likes—and your dislikes. Give him or her selections for your first dance, mother-son dance, and your last dance, but also let him or her know if there are any songs that are in the no-spin zone. You might think now that there's nothing you wouldn't mind—and then find yourself doing the chicken dance in a tux. Stick to light, ambient music during dinner; wait until the meal is done to have your band or DJ crank it up.

Inquiring minds want to know: Can you hear them play live at another event? How long do they need for setup? How much space is necessary? What will they wear? Are there any travel expenses? Do they take breaks? Will they play live or prerecorded music during these breaks?

Watch for: The ol' switcheroo. When using a large entertainment company, make sure your contract states that you will have the exact musicians you saw or heard. Too many times, couples have been stunned to find that the bandleader they met with (and adored) isn't the one performing at their wedding.

PHOTOGRAPHY

Most couples devote a large portion of their budget to the photographer. Besides the visions in your head, your pictures will be a lasting memory of your wedding day. Find a photographer you're comfortable with—remember that he or she will be shooting you and your lady for an average of eight hours! That's a lot of face time.

Your options: The two main approaches are a candid, photojournalistic style (lots of black-and-whites—they might catch you making that funny face of yours) and traditional, posed photography (the whole family standing in front of a background). A mix of both will deliver a nice blend of artsy photos and traditional pics of the wedding's key players that your parents will like. These days, many wedding photographers shoot digitally, citing comparable film quality yet faster turnaround times. Digital capabilities also offer the photographer the ability to see the results immediately and make necessary adjustments to lighting or position on the spot.

Key points: Time is money when it comes to photography. Decide when you want your photographer to start—they always capture the bride's final transformation and get some portraits of her, but do you also want pictures of you and your main men during those anxiety-filled getting-ready moments? If so, try to schedule those shots just before the ceremony—and stick to your timeline. If the clock goes into OT, it's going to cost you about $400 per hour. Make sure to consider the overall package you want: The majority of wedding photographers do a 60-40 split between black-and-white and color, respectively, so speak up if you prefer one style. Ask to see photos of weddings

PHOTOGRAPHY STYLES

A. Candid Photography

B. Posed Photography

that took place at the same time as yours will. He or she may excel only in candlelight, for example. Finally, check out the album options. Many photographers own your negatives, which means you'll have to purchase them for a hefty fee or get an album (at an additional cost, naturally) through the photographer.

Inquiring minds want to know: What is the photographer's philosophy about shooting weddings? Is he or she open to direction—as in a list of must-take shots? How does the photographer determine price—by the hour, number of pictures, developing time, or a combo? Does he or she edit the proofs? Is there an assistant? What's the turnaround time?

Watch for: Extreme personalities. A shooter who is really sweet may not have the gusto to organize your rowdy family and friends for the formal photos. A photographer with a commandeering style may make guests uncomfortable and unwilling to smile. And a fine-art fanatic may not honor your request for formal photos in the way you expect (headless body shots, perhaps?).

→ → → **TIPS ON TIPPING**

Yes, you'll be handing out plenty of tips on your big day. So who are these lucky recipients of your generosity? And how much do you give? We'll begin with the first person you may encounter and then walk through the rest of the day.

⦿ Wedding coordinator: No matter how intricate or basic their jobs are, they usually won't be expecting a tip. If you'd like to show your appreciation, you can include a monetary thank-you in a note, or perhaps send a little gift after the wedding.

⦿ Officiant: It's traditional for the best man to hand over this tip, which should be between $100 and $200. If you're getting married in a house of worship, you may be expected to donate a percentage of your total wedding cost—so if your wedding is running $20,000, a $2,000 donation will be gratefully accepted. However, if you don't belong to this church or synagogue and you didn't have a lot of involvement with the officiant, you can choose to contribute a lower amount.

● Transportation: If all goes smoothly with your transport to the party (and we're sure it will), add about 15 to 20 percent of the total to the bill, unless gratuity is already included.

● Parking attendants/valets: If you're providing parking services for guests, give the supervisor a tip for the attendants ahead of time. Calculate about $1 per car. And don't forget to spread the word that you've taken care of the gratuity so your guests don't feel compelled to slip the guy a buck.

● Coatroom and restroom attendants: If this gratuity is not factored into the bill already, $.50 to $1 per guest should suffice.

● Musicians (ceremony and reception): Tipping the musicians is completely optional. If you do decide to slip them some cash, calculate $20 to $25 for each member.

● Photographer or videographer: This is completely optional. If you're paying top dollar for these services, they shouldn't be expecting a gratuity. However, a thank-you in the form of cash is always appreciated, especially if the photographer or videographer doesn't own his or her own studio. Estimate $20 to $25.

● Banquet manager or maitre d': This is where it's very important to check your contract to find out whether you're already paying a service charge. If gratuity is not included in your total bill, figure from $200 to $300 as a tip, depending on the size of your wedding. This amount should go to the person in charge of your reception; if there's more than one person in charge, divide the gratuity among them.

● Caterer and waitstaff: If your reception isn't being held at a hotel or club, it's nice to show you appreciate all of their efforts working in a less-than-kitchen-friendly space. Figure the tip according to the number of waiters—decide on a dollar amount per server (let's say $20) and then multiply by the number of servers working at your reception, plus some for the catering manager.

● Bartenders: Once again, it's time to scrutinize the bill. Sometimes at hotels and clubs a service charge is included in the liquor bill. If there isn't one, leaving 10 percent of the total liquor bill for the bartenders is a nice gesture. Try to find the head bartender when handing over the cash.

Now, here's some good news: there are some people you don't have to tip. The owner of a business won't expect a tip; instead you should tip the people working for that owner. In addition, the florist, baker, and bridal shop employees will not be expecting a gratuity, nor will the invitation or party rental companies. However, thank-you notes are always universally and eternally appreciated.

STYLE SELECTIONS

After you've hired the heavy hitters, most of the remaining vendor decisions will revolve around the anticipated look of the wedding. You may feel like this isn't your strong suit; if so, feel free to skip ahead. However, a great wedding is one whose elements (flowers, cake, invitations) reflect the personal style of *both* the bride and groom. Take a read through the following items to give you a sense of what the choices are, and how you might contribute to some of the decisions. You don't want your guys calling and giving you a hard time about the hot-pink (what?!) invites. If you really don't want to get involved with these style decisions at all, be clear about it up front–that way your bride will know she can just run with it. But be forewarned: you can't say later that you don't like the choices. Consider establishing a rule that she must let you know about the overall look and feel of a major decision before it hits the presses (or flower market or bakery).

FLOWERS AND DECOR

When your bride walks down the aisle, all eyes will be on her and her bouquet. Flower vendors might hold zero interest for you, but a little education won't sting. Visit flower shops at least six months before the wedding and ask to see their photos from previous weddings.

Your options: Your vendor decision will be based on how much work there is to be done. If you're looking for traditional floral touches, find a local florist or reputable flower shop to handle the bouquets, boutonnieres, and floral arrangements for the reception tables and the ceremony space. If you want a full-scale floral design of the space, look for a floral event designer to handle the job. It will cost you, but your entire room will be transformed into a fresh flower utopia. When it comes to style, choose between classic wedding blooms (such as white roses and calla lilies) or creative floral installations with things like green apples in the bases of vases bursting with cherry blossoms.

Key points: Make sure your florist is someone whose taste you find, well, tasteful. Discuss any specific flowers that are musts (or mustn'ts). If the estimate seems out of your budget, ask how you might get a similar effect with lower-priced flowers and greens. You can pick the florist's brain about what will be in season and therefore less expensive on your date.

Inquiring minds want to know: Has the florist done weddings at your ceremony or reception site before? If not, is he or she able to check out the venue prior to the wedding? Will you ultimately be working the florist herself or her floral assistants? Where will he or she deliver the bouquets and boutonnieres? Will the florist be involved in site setup?

Watch for: Wilting petals. If your wedding will be in a very humid climate—especially if it's outdoors—certain flowers may droop before you officially tie the knot. Also ask what kinds of flowers have staying power but little scent so guests don't faint from their cloying aromas. Leave that to your cologne. (Just kidding.)

INVITATIONS

They all look the same to you, right? Get ready for an education. Rich handmade papers and printing techniques such as engraving and letterpress can make invitations cost more than a phat new TV. To be ready for mailing at the two-month mark, start scoping out invitations five months ahead to allow for printing time and calligraphy for the envelopes.

Your options: Invitations are guests' first introduction to your wedding, so the look should represent your couple style and the party's feel—classic white linen with black script for the traditional couple, colored stock with metallic block letters for a funky pair. You can order existing designs from a catalog (there are hundreds to choose from, in all different price ranges), or create a custom design with a graphic artist (ask around for recommendations or place an ad in a local art school's newspaper).

Key points: What you really need to concern yourself with is wording. Before you print the invitations, discuss the language with all parties. The safest bet is to include both sets of parents' names, particularly if your parents are contributing—or state that you're extending the invitation "together with their parents." And be prepared for multiple nights spent not just stuffing envelopes but also adding layers of protective tissue, inserting response cards, and so on. Depending on what you'll include with your invitation, you may have three or four pieces that need to be put together. Pitch in, but let your fiancée guide you through it once first. There are rules for this too (hint: from the bottom up, it's D-I-R-RSVP–direction card, invitation, reception card, response card). Also, be sure to order twenty-five extra invitations and envelopes in case of lost mail or unforeseen accidents.

Inquiring minds want to know: Does the stationer do custom designs? What about calligraphy for the addresses? Can you change the wording of invitations in the sample books? Will you be able to see a proof before it's printed? What is the expected printing time?

Watch for: DIY invitations. Your fiancée may think that you'll save a ton of money by re-creating the hand-pressed leaf invitations she fell in love with at the stationery store, but costly supplies and the time and frustration involved are often not worth the extra pennies–especially if you have more than one hundred invitees. Trust us. After a long day on the job, do you really want to be hot-gluing tiny leaves to a piece of paper? Unless you're an art school alum, this situation could be a recipe for disaster.

FONT STYLES

A. Script

B. Serif

These notices, usually sent six months before the wedding day (more if it's a destination affair), let your guests know about your big day. Here's how to prepare for the mailing.

→ Include the date, time, and place of the event (of course), as well as any suggested lodging and travel arrangements.

→ Negotiate travel deals. Many hotels are accustomed to blocking rooms at a discounted rate for weddings, so this shouldn't be too difficult a task.

→ Figure out which airline has a hub near your wedding locale and call to see if you can get a group discount. If the airline's ticket office isn't too far from where you live, you might want to go in person.

Note: These days it's perfectly acceptable to send save-the-dates via e-mail. Just be sure your parents' friends have Internet access—you may have to make special phone calls to them if they don't.

CAKE

There's more to a cake than taste. Seriously. The look should match the mood you're trying to create. Enlist a reputable cake baker early in the process (six to eight months ahead), then finalize the style around the three-month mark. The cost will depend on how many people you're feeding, since bakers often charge per slice. But here's a well-known secret of fake cakes: The bottom tier of a wedding cake is real for the cutting, while the top layers are actually decorated Styrofoam. You can then buy a regular sheet cake for additional serving. Genius, no?

Key points: You definitely want to be a part of the cake tastings. (It's free cake!) If your taste buds don't agree with your fiancée's, consider ordering layers in different flavors. And many brides placate the groom with his own cake. (Can you believe it? Something just for you!) The groom's cake is traditionally a darker, heavier cake, like chocolate, and has a wackier theme design that reflects his job or hobby (we know of one groom who had a cake shaped like the Golden Gate Bridge in honor of his hometown).

Inquiring minds want to know: What ingredients are used? How far in advance are cakes prepared? Will the cake designer work with your florist if you so desire? Do different flavors or fillings come at different prices? What is the delivery process?

Watch for: Crazy creations. You can't read a cake by its looks, so don't sacrifice taste for a labor-intensive look. Depending on the design's intricacy, your baker may need to start work days ahead of time to get the job done. Cost will be based on the amount of work entailed in decorating. Also, the construction should be able to withstand the rigors of transportation—a fallen cake is never a pleasant sight.

TRANSPORTATION

About two months before the wedding, start looking for transportation companies that specialize in weddings. The cost will depend on how many vehicles are in your fleet and how far you need to go. These vendors tend to work hourly, but expect minimums—no one is going to give up a whole Saturday night to drive you for one hour to the ceremony.

Your options: Classic cars, stretch limos, or unusual rides. Your arrival and departure are great ways to spice things up. New limo options include SUV limos, Hummer limos, and luxury car limos. Black cars say chic, while white is a classic (borderline cheesy) color for wedding wheels. Or add humor and individuality with a horse and buggy, trolley, sleigh, canoe, or even rickshaw. You could even ask a friend or family member to lend that vintage Mustang hidden in the garage. Also, think about hiring buses or vans to transport key family members to and from the ceremony and reception.

Key points: If you decide to have the photographer ride with you for paparazzi shots, make sure your wheels can accommodate the photographer in addition to your bride's big gown. And don't leave your attendants to hitchhike. Take a headcount of your wedding party and important family members that need a lift, and determine how many cars (or a van or bus) you'll need to hire. Transportation is often an obvious area for cutting costs. Shop around for the best price. Many limo companies jack up prices for weddings, so try to negotiate. Prices vary from city to city, so make sure to ask friends who married in your area for suggestions. Find out if you can arrange for a pickup and drop-off—making drivers wait only increases costs.

TRANSPORTATION OPTIONS

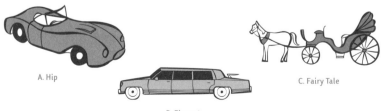

A. Hip

B. Elegant

C. Fairy Tale

Watch for: Being stranded. A week before the wedding, finalize travel arrangements and e-mail your car company with a pickup and drop-off schedule so there's no mistaking where they need to go. Inform them of any traffic concerns (access roads that are busy during high season) and create a full contact sheet with everyone's phone numbers.

→ → → **GETTING GUESTS AROUND TOWN**

If you have many out-of-town guests staying at locations not within walking distance of the ceremony and reception, you'll need to help coordinate their travel to and from the wedding. You have several options:

1 Carpool: Make arrangements for friends and family with cars to make pick-ups and drop-offs.

2 Taxis: If they're easy to come by in your area, you can hire a fleet of taxis to pick up guests. If guests cover the cost of the cabs, it could lighten your load–but you'll need to coordinate the effort.

3 Hired transport: Vans (nine to fifteen people) or buses (forty to sixty people) are great options when there's a gaggle of guests to transport. You can often hire these vehicles from the same car company where you're getting your own wedding wheels.

4 If you aren't providing guest transportation or everyone is local, make sure ample parking is available at your reception site and consider hiring parking attendants to run the show.

VIDEOGRAPHY

You want the guy with the lights and camera to show up–you just don't want to know he's there. Fortunately, given today's small, packable digital equipment, it's easy for videographers to be unobtrusive. Since photographers and videographers often work together, you may want to ask your shooter for a referral and consider hiring both at the same time.

Your options: Choose between bare-bones coverage and a slick edit with all the bells and whistles. Like everything, you'll pay for a more polished product. Also, style is a supreme consideration. Are you looking for a documentary feel–just what happened, shot very realistically–or an MTV-video version of your wedding packed with interesting angles and quick shots?

Key points: Find someone who shares your vision and won't drive you crazy with corniness. If you don't find that Muzak-scored montage sample moving, it's time to move on. If the quick shots and quirky angles in that budding experimental filmmaker's sample make you dizzy, consider hiring someone else.

Inquiring minds want to know: Has the videographer done many weddings? What is his or her approach? Has he or she worked with your photographer before, or filmed a wedding at your site? What is the equipment arrangement? Can you get a DVD instead of VHS? What is the final product?

Watch for: Rules. Don't assume your videographer will have total artistic freedom during your ceremony. Some sanctuaries do not allow bright lights and may place restrictions on your cameraman's movements—check the rules with your officiant before you get ready for your close-up.

→ → → **INCORPORATING YOU IN THE WEDDING**

Getting married doesn't mean losing your individuality. While it seems the bulk of the affair reflects her tastes (a.k.a. your new tastes), there are ways to put your man-stamp on the party. Though she might not agree totally with your suggestion to hire an AC/DC cover band, you two can work on a way to incorporate your idea into the event (like having the band you do end up hiring play a few of your favorite AC/DC songs). Here are some other ideas:

- Have a little fun with the formalwear. Pick out great cuff links for you and the guys (a no-brainer gift idea) and perhaps your favorite designer's ties. Or honor your heritage with traditional wedding wear specific to that county: Scottish kilts, Mexican *guayaberas*, or English morning coats.

- Suggest a theme. Love to sail? Present the idea of a yacht or sailboat as an inspiration for the invitations and favors. If your fiancée wants to keep it simple, insist on a groom's cake of your own design.

- Feed them your favorites. Is there a special dish that you could simply die for? See if your caterer can incorporate it into the meal. Love doughnuts? Hand 'em out at the end of the night—they'll do double-duty as a sweet treat and alcohol soaker!

- Name your tables. If your fiancée's game, name the tables after your favorite cities or pastimes.

- Create a cocktail. Are Jack and Gingers your thing? Serve them to the crowd.

- Write your vows. There's no better expression of you.

ABOVE AND BEYOND

See how much there is to consider when planning a wedding? Now you understand why your fiancée has turned into an obsessive-compulsive questioner. But you're not off the hook yet—you still need to book your honeymoon and register for gifts. It'll be worth it in the end!

THE HONEYMOON

Perhaps more than the wedding, the honeymoon has always been your fantasy. This is your hard-earned reward for enduring all that stressful planning. The catch? It needs to be planned—usually about six months before the wedding. Putting together a honeymoon isn't too hard, since destinations are often clamoring for honeymooners. And it's a nice way to ease your fiancée's burden and to make sure you have a great time.

Travel Documents

Your options: Even if you're both thinking beach, you'll need to settle on one place. Hawaii, Aruba, Fiji? But sand isn't a honeymoon requirement. Maybe you want a week at a ski chalet, a few days to take a bite out of the Big Apple, or a two-week tour of the Greek isles.

Key points: Schedule your trip for a time when it's convenient. There's no law that says you have to take your honeymoon right after the wedding. Pick a time that works with both of your schedules. And if you have friends and family in town who want to hang out with you post-wedding, wait at least a couple of days before you take off. Talk to friends about their honeymoon experiences and surf the Web to see what trips might fit into your budget. Yes, like everything else, you need a honeymoon budget. Consider using a travel agent to get really great deals, and inform hotels of your honeymoon status—it may get you some complimentary champagne.

Surprise your sweetie with some unexpected perks, once you get to your chosen spot. See if there's a spa on the premises or a reputable one nearby. Schedule a morning massage or a manicure and pedicure. She'll melt on the spot. Or if you know she loves to ride horses, contact a local tour guide and plan a day trip. It's the little things that count—remember that, now and forever.

Inquiring minds want to know: What's your destination's average temperature for the month you're traveling? Is it swarming with children? What's the best way to get around? Do you need special visas or immunizations?

Watch for: Airport troubles. Remember to use her maiden name when making arrangements, unless you're positive she'll have time to change her documents before you travel.

REGISTERING FOR GIFTS

Most men might name this section "The Most Tortuous Shopping Experience of My Life." Reality check: you want gifts you need and like—and a registry is simply a massive wish list that people will actually use to buy you gifts.

Your options: Endless. Well, almost. More stores than ever have gift registries, making it possible to register for practically anything, from computers to chainsaws to camping equipment. Traditionally, here is what should be on your list.

◉ Cookware: Check your kitchen inventory, and then fill in the blanks with quality cookware including knives, pots and pans, a mixer, a blender, a food processor, a toaster, bakeware, cookie sheets, a coffee-maker, a coffee grinder, and other cool kitchen gadgets. The latest trend is for couples to pick and choose different pans in different materials (say one pan in cast iron, another in stainless steel) to build your very own *batterie de cuisine.*

A. Stock Pot

B. Frying Pan

C. Sauce Pan

◉ Glassware: Vases, wineglasses, barware, everyday drinking glasses, and shot glasses, of course. It's a good idea to register for extra glasses in case of breakage or if you throw lots of parties. If you decide on crystal glasses, include red and white wineglasses, water goblets, champagne flutes, and double old-fashioned glasses.

A. Wineglass

B. Highball

C. Double Old-Fashioned

● China: Decide between fine china and everyday ware, although you might choose to register for both if you've got a big guest list (with deep pockets). You should register for eight to twelve place settings of each. Your fiancée will probably lead the picking-a-pattern charge, but remind her to play it safe—pink roses have no business being on your plates.

● Flatware: Sterling silver or stainless steel. It's really a money thing.

● Bedding and bath: If you're inclined toward an update, pick out nice, new gender-neutral bed linens and bath towels. (Note: When your gal starts going ga-ga over thread counts, know that the higher the number the better.)

● Guy-friendly items: Luggage, barbecue grill, lawn mower, wine storage, electronics, camera, tools, a tent . . . you're limited only by the store's stock and your imagination!

Key points: Divide and conquer. Choose the areas you want to be involved in. If you don't really care what flatware or dinnerware she prefers, give her carte blanche. But you may want to come along for the ride when it comes time to select the coffeemaker and blender. If you're smart, you'll do your research. If you're willing to pick out pots and pans, maybe she'll give you free rein in the electronics department. And remember, wielding a scanner gun is fun. (She may even let you control it.) Just keep your manly urges in check so you don't gratuitously scan multiple mixers.

Inquiring minds want to know: What are the return policies? Can we choose different shipping addresses for before and after the wedding? How do we manage the registry? Can guests purchase items online? What is the policy on holding gifts until after the wedding?

Watch for: Expensive goods. Don't lose focus and register for all big-ticket items. You need to choose products in a wide range of prices to accommodate all budgets. Also, you'll want to have a good mix of appropriate engagement, shower, and wedding presents available.

THE VIRTUAL GROOM: Hit the Web to set up a gift fund online. The Knot's create-a-gift service allows you to basically create your own registry. You can ask for anything—from a down payment on a house to your honeymoon. Guests can then purchase gift checks in dollar increments that go toward your hearts' desire.

BEST MAN
10

USHER
7

GROOMSMAN
22

RING BEARER
00

ON your wedding day, you won't be up at the altar alone. Besides your bride (and the officiant, if we're getting technical), you'll have a team of gents to support you—then and throughout the whole process. Many are born into it, and some are chosen. While your fiancée deliberates over which of her closest friends or siblings will walk before her down the aisle, you may pick your groomsmen without a second thought: your college roommate, your brother, her brother, and your childhood pal, perhaps. While the decision may seem like a no-brainer to you, consider how responsible these guys are. Can you trust each one to show up at the church on time? These are also the men who will plan your bachelor party. Beware.

Here, we present an overview of the entire cast and crew and explain how everyone fits into the wedding-party puzzle. We'll give you the goods on when to choose your best man and groomsmen, and how to keep them informed and manage their financial expectations. We also delve deeper into the roles of the best man, groomsmen, and ushers, with tips on making them aware of their duties. This chapter will provide you with everything you need to know to keep your guys organized and on your side.

THE LINEUP

You don't have to rush out and pick your wedding party the second you get engaged. You can ask the obvious candidates (your brother for best man, for instance) right away, and make your final decisions later–but no more than a month after you're engaged. The guys should definitely know their roles in your wedding before the engagement party and be prepared to pitch in. If you're not comfortable writing your friends sentimental notes asking them to be in your wedding party, stick with the telephone. Or take them out for drinks or a round of golf. This may be the perfect way to introduce fellows who may not know each other very well–or at least break the ice before the bachelor party. Here's your groom's list of important players:

Best man: Literally, your best man. (See the facing page for more on him.)

Groomsmen: Your other stand-up guys. (More on choosing them on page 80.)

Ushers: Responsible for helping guests to their seats during the ceremony and often running out last minute for a forgotten item. They're reliable, good friends you want to bestow an honor on (other than the role of groomsman). (Read more on page 83.)

Here's what you need to know about the rest of the players.

Maid of honor: A complement to the best man, this best woman is chosen by your bride from among siblings and friends. She's the bride's biggest supporter in the days leading up to the wedding and a most important person on the day of the event. If married, she's called the matron of honor.

Bridesmaids: Like groomsmen, these honored women stand up at the ceremony with your fiancée and are typically her close friends or sisters.

Usherettes: The female equivalents of ushers, they often give out programs at the ceremony.

Flower girl: She leads the wedding procession. This is a great post for a special niece or little sister. Invite her to come up near the front when you cut the cake. She'll never forget it.

Ring bearer: Ask your favorite little man. Before the ceremony, introduce him to the groomsmen to help him feel more comfortable, since being around a bunch of older guys can be intimidating, especially if he hardly knows them.

Readers: These VIPs usually read poems or passages during the ceremony. This is a nice way to include relatives or family friends who might otherwise get overlooked.

THE BEST MAN

HIS ROLE

Having a best man originated in the days when a man would literally kidnap his bride. When her family came to rescue her, the best man was there—a loyal, trusted friend the groom could totally rely upon, ready to help out in a fight should they try taking her back. Today, the same holds true (minus the kidnapping part). The best man needs to be responsible and have taste (remember, he plans the bachelor party). The more dependable he is, the more tasks you can pile on him. His top tasks? Walking the maid of honor down the aisle, making the first toast, and wrangling out important details.

WHOM TO CHOOSE

Pick someone who's an active part of your—and your fiancée's—life. (The night before your wedding is not the time to discover you and your best friend from high school no longer have much in common.) The best choice is someone with a comfortable presence who'll stand beside you before, during, and after the ceremony—someone who won't forget the ring or show up with a raging hangover or hit on your bride's seventeen-year-old sister. If you have a brother, he should be on your shortlist—in fact, tradition says he should be your best man. If he's not the only one you want as your best man, why not opt for two best men? You can split duties between them (see page 78 for a list) to keep the peace.

What if you make a choice and then change your mind because he's slacking off, turning out to be irresponsible, and not returning your calls? The bad news is that once you've asked, you can't un-ask. You'll actually have to talk to him about your concerns. If he's not responsive or simply not getting the job done, call in your reserves—see which best-man duties your other groomsmen can handle.

WHAT'S REQUIRED OF HIM

Before you both agree that this is the role for him, talk about what being a best man entails. The best man is expected to assist in the planning, pick out the formalwear with the groom, ensure that the groomsmen get their attire on time, hand out boutonnieres, take care of the rings, organize the ushers, escort the maid of honor down the aisle, sign the marriage license, handle payments for people like the officiant and the organist, hand out tips for service providers such as the coat-check attendants and servers (if not covered in your catering contract), make the first toast (read our tips on page 79), serve as MC if necessary, decorate the getaway car, and make sure all the formalwear is returned.

Phew. Seems like a lot, right? There's also a financial burden to consider. Tux rental. That Vegas bachelor party. Traditionally, you don't pay for a thing. (But be a good groom and offer to cover your airfare and hotel accommodations.) The bachelor party is his responsibility (see our sidebar on the basics, right). For all these reasons, you need to make sure he's up to the challenge.

It's your last hurrah—your night of wild revelry with the guys who got you to where you are now. Here's the scoop on your bon voyage to bachelorhood.

When: This party can take place anytime from three months before the big day to the night before the rehearsal dinner. You may want to choose a time at least a few weeks before the wedding, so you won't be too run down (read: hungover) on the day of. Also, if the male-bonding event freaks out your bride, it's a good idea to give her plenty of time to calm down before you both walk down that aisle.

What: Sorry, you don't really get to decide—your wedding party is in charge of this fete. But you can send a message to your best man. If you really don't want strippers, say so. If you've always dreamed of Vegas (and your guys can swing it), speak up. They can surprise you with the specifics, but it's a good idea to give guidelines—especially if your best man is a notorious ladies' man. Some ideas include a fishing trip, golf day, two-day camping excursion, bike trip, steak dinner, or weekend in New York City. As long as you've got the guys together, you're guaranteed a good time.

Who goes: Yes, you do get to decide this. Typically, your wedding party is included, and any other very close friends and family members who didn't make the groomsman cut. Consider asking your dad (and your bride's dad), if you think it's appropriate—or if they'd feel comfortable at such an event. The bachelor party can be big or small—hang with just the groomsmen or thirty of your closest friends. It really depends on what you want.

The aftermath: If you share absolutely nothing with your fiancée about your bachelor party, she'll suspect the worst—even if you do nothing wrong. Let her know where you stayed or ate dinner so she doesn't think you're hiding info. Be prepared for the third degree. If strippers are involved, always say that they were unattractive and that the strip joint was kind of nasty. Don't say you can't remember anything, even if you really can't—that will definitely make her imagination run wild.

Share this general list of responsibilities with him so he knows what being the best man is all about. Help your main man out and photocopy his list of duties, below. He may call you corny, but he'll thank you in the end.

Best Man's Cheat Sheet

- Attend all pre-wedding functions, like the engagement party and rehearsal dinner. If the shower's coed, he should help the maid of honor pull it together.
- Know the stores where the couple is registered and help spread the word.
- Plan the bachelor party (with help from the groomsmen).
- Help choose tuxedos and wear the monkey suit without complaining about it.
- Coordinate the groomsmen's rentals (including measurements, payments, pickups, and returns); pay for his own tux rental.
- Listen to groom vent about the bride or wedding planning without getting cynical.
- Coordinate the groomsmen's wedding transportation (and lodging, if necessary).
- Stand by the groom during the ceremony.
- Sign the marriage certificate after the wedding.
- Hand the officiant his or her fee after the ceremony.
- Take part in the receiving line, if you're having one.
- Kick off the dinner portion of the reception with a toast.
- Collect and keep secure any gift envelopes the couple receives at the wedding.
- Have cash in hand for emergency tipping or bribing.
- Help clear people from the reception room and lead guests to the after-party (if there is one).
- Drive the couple to their honeymoon suite or to the airport for their honeymoon.
- Be supportive throughout the process and always make the groom laugh.

Have you thought about asking your best man to serve as the master of cere-monies for the wedding? We're not talking about getting up with the band and singing a Sinatra cover—we mean directing the entertainment. Bandleaders often take on the job, but having your best man run the show, introducing speakers and each part of the program (like when it's time to cut the cake), may be more personal. This would be a good fit if he's got charisma; if he's shy, the added stress could push him over the edge. If your main man is up for it, here are great tips to help him do it right.

→ Let him know that the best strategy is to keep his comments short, sweet, and sincere—unless he knows he is very funny.

→ Provide him with the schedule for the day—when everything happens, who's doing what, and background info on all the toast makers (so he can say: "Next up, the maid of honor, who has known the bride since she was two!").

→ Suggest that he test out the microphone beforehand and get comfortable using it. That high-pitched feedback is a friend to no one. He can get every-one's attention by gently tapping his finger on the mike and waiting for every-one to focus. He can also tap his glass with a fork to bring the room to a halt. Ah . . . the power of the clink.

→ Remind him to keep his commentary clean and in good taste. When announc-ing that the bar is open, it's not a good idea to direct the comment at your notoriously drunk uncle.

→ Tell him to have notes ready. It's the best antidote for that lethal combo of nerves and excitement.

→ Explain the etiquette. When it's time for his toast, he should raise his glass and say something quick (under three minutes), personal, and sincere—but most of all, appropriate for the audience. No need to regale with bachelor-party tales (he can save those for the john).

THE GROOMSMEN

T he guys you choose to be with you on this day are your real boys—the ones who have always had your back. The first rule of thumb? Don't talk about your wedding party among friends until you've made your final decision. While most people understand that not everyone can be in the wedding, it's possible to hurt feelings and ruffle a few feathers if you're not perfectly genteel. Participating in a wedding is an honor and should be taken seriously.

CHOOSING YOUR CREW

Your best buddies, college roommates, brothers, cousins, or even long-lost elementary school friends may be ripe for the role. Consider all the issues:

Family: Don't forget about your fiancée when making your decision. More specifically, don't forget about her family. Your bride may have her heart set on her little brother being a groomsman. As long as you can stand the guy,

Dress Shoes

you'll do well to play along. The opposite is also true: if you want your sister to serve as bridesmaid, your bride will probably agree. But you don't have to stick with tradition. If you two are open-minded, your sister might stand on your side—in an official groomsman role—while your fiancée's brother stands on her side (see our sidebar on page 82 for more on the new gender rules).

Size constraints: Keep in mind that even if your fiancée selects her thirteen closest ladies to stand up for her, you're not required to bring your own baker's dozen. While many couples are sticklers for altar symmetry, there's no rule that says you must match groomsman for bridesmaid. Feel free to choose as many or as few men as you like. Keeping the ratio even can help for ceremony purposes, but it's not required. And your cousin probably won't mind a bit if he has to stroll down the aisle with a hot bridesmaid on each arm.

Lack of enthusiasm: Your groomsmen will have to be available for tuxedo fittings, pre-wedding parties, and the good ol' bachelor party. If they live far away, will this be a financial strain for them? Don't feel dejected if your chosen few don't leap for joy at the prospect—just make sure they really do want to be a part of the party.

SETTING EXPECTATIONS

Groomsmen often also act as ushers and help seat guests. Besides greeting people in front of the ceremony site and escorting those drop-dead-gorgeous bridesmaids down the aisle after the service, their general role is to help the best man organize the groom's side of things, make sure they look presentable, and show up on time. They'll also be expected to keep the party going, dance with single females, and decorate the getaway car. Keep your guys on their toes with this detailed checklist of what's required of them.

Groomsmen's Cheat Sheet

- ◉ Attend all pre-wedding functions (engagement party, coed shower, rehearsal dinner).
- ◉ Know the stores where the couple is registered and help spread the news.
- ◉ Help the best man plan the bachelor party.
- ◉ Pay rental fees for their own tuxes and shoes.
- ◉ Get their measurements to the groom on time.
- ◉ Pick up their tuxes at the requested time.
- ◉ Wear appropriate-colored socks.
- ◉ Conspire with the entire bridal party to decorate the honeymoon getaway car.
- ◉ Politely usher guests to their seats.
- ◉ Stand with the groom during the ceremony.
- ◉ Point confused guests in the right direction, whether to the bathroom or the gift table.
- ◉ Make sure bridesmaids and other single female guests have dance partners.
- ◉ Help lug gifts and couple's personal accoutrements after the reception.

In true seventh-grade style, weddings often seem like boys on one side, girls on the other. But it doesn't have to be this way. If your best friend happens to be your sister (or another female), ask her to be your best woman. Or a groomsgirl. Seriously. She can wear a black or dark-colored dress in lieu of a suit, or a dress to match those of the bridesmaids, if she'd prefer. As long as the woman isn't an ex and your wife-to-be has given her approval, it's perfectly OK. If this somewhat unconventional arrangement raises a few eyebrows, just explain that you want the people you're tightest with nearby—no matter the gender.

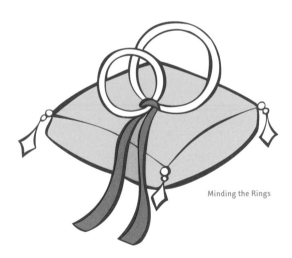

Minding the Rings

THE USHERS

I f you decide to have only a best man or a few groomsmen but want to include other friends or male relatives, get them in on the action by asking them to be ushers. That way you can include everyone, and avoid bitter backlash.

THEIR ROLE

In general, you need one usher for every fifty guests. These honored guys often receive a boutonniere similar to the groomsmen's and, plain and simple, are in charge of seating. This is also a good role for junior groomsmen—young cousins or siblings who don't fit into the task-heavy groomsman role.

Ushers should attend the ceremony rehearsal in order to understand the seating arrangements and let you point out key players. Or you could tell honored guests to instruct the ushers where they should be seated, or you could even pass out pew cards for the key family members to hand to the ushers. Once the ceremony gets underway, it may be a good idea for one of them to stand in the back of the ceremony space to seat any naughty latecomers.

Ceremony Programs

CHOOSING USHERS

Make sure everyone you chose for this role is polite and responsible. It's often a good idea to have an usher from each family who'll recognize key people (like your bride's grandma and your great-aunt) and place them in their proper seats of honor. For ushers not in your immediate clan, you'll need to spell out who's who.

INCLUSION IDEAS

Ushers sometimes feel like stepchildren—they often don't know what their role in the wedding should be. Basically, ushers should be treated like groomsmen: they are invited to pre-wedding parties, they sport the same attire as the groomsmen, attend the bachelor party, and they help out with any wedding-day must-dos. When it comes to formal photos, though, it's best to stick with core bridal party shots and a separate usher pose.

Usher Cheat Sheet

- Attend all pre-wedding functions (engagement party, coed shower, rehearsal dinner).
- Know the stores where the couple is registered and help spread the news.
- Pay rental fees for their own tuxes and shoes.
- Get measurements to the groom on time.
- Pick up their tuxes at the requested time.
- Wear appropriate-colored socks.
- Learn the names and faces of the key people to be seated in the honor rows.
- Politely usher guests to their seats.
- Stand at the back of the ceremony space to seat latecomers.

FITTING IN FAMILY

After all these pages, it may seem like these guys are your only allies. But don't forget about other key wedding players like, uh, your family.

MOM AND DAD

Give your parents a special floral accent (corsage for mom, boutonniere for dad) that coordinates with those of the bride's mom and dad. Don't forget to make your mom feel important on this day. One obvious way to do this is the mother-son dance. Make it extra special and have the dance early in the night to one of her favorite songs. Your father should take on the role of good-humored cohost. Ask him if he would usher some of his friends to their seats at the reception (promise him a celebratory cigar on the terrace when the party is over).

GRANDMA AND GRANDPA

While your grandparents don't have official titles or roles, they'll be thrilled to be at your wedding—and it's important for you to think of a way to make them feel honored. Consider presenting them with a corsage and boutonniere too. Aside from reserving their seating at the ceremony, ask your officiant to mention how happy you are to have your grandparents with you to celebrate. You could also suggest a grandparent dance at the reception.

SPECIAL GUESTS

Besides your aunts and uncles and siblings and cousins who are not part of the wedding party, there are probably some exceptional individuals whom you'd like to give a little extra wedding-day love. Think about older people who have helped shape your life—your mother's best friend from high schoool who has become your surrogate aunt; your grandmother's brother; your college mentor. When weddings become so focused on "family," these bride- and groom-rated VIPs may get overlooked. Here are ten ways they can contribute that will make them feel part of the in crowd:

→ Give a special toast at the rehearsal dinner (especially to honor those important persons who have recently passed)
→ Light an honor candle at the ceremony
→ Read a passage or poem during the ceremony
→ Hold the chuppah at a Jewish ceremony
→ Sign your marriage license or *ketubah*
→ Be a part of the receiving line
→ Singing a song or playing an instrument at the reception
→ Saying a blessing over the food at the reception
→ Have a special dance with the groom
→ Host the post-wedding brunch

MANAGING YOUR TEAM

Unlike you, your groomsmen probably won't have a fiancée (or this book) to keep them on top of all their duties. Your smartest plan? Photocopy the lists we've provided in these pages, and make the best man your ultimate organizer. Communicating with your guys will ensure everything goes smoothly. The first order of business: set up a groomsmen e-mail list on your computer. So many details need to be shared over the next months—from the date of the rehearsal dinner to tuxedo styles to great airfares—and you'll want to make sure no one is left out of the loop. Use these handy formats and feel free to make them your own.

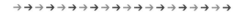

E-mail #1: The Meet and Greet
To: Groomsmen, Ushers
cc: The Bride
From: The Groom
Subject: Contact info for the wedding party

To my main men,
You've all accepted my invitation to stand up for me at my wedding, for better or for worse! Here's a little about each guy, with contact information so you can start planning my bachelor party.
Best Man: My little brother John Doe. John's still partying hard at Booze U, so be wary of his bachelor party ideas. Keep it mellow, John. Contact info: (555) 555-5555; john doe@booze.edu.
Groomsman #1: Blah Blah.
Groomsman #2: Blah Blah.
Thanks, guys! It's gonna be a wild year.

E-mail #2: Save the Date
To: Groomsmen, Ushers
cc: The Bride
From: The Groom
Subject: It's really happening!

We've booked a place. The wedding will be held at 2:00 P.M. on Saturday, October 11, 2006, at the Swanky Hotel, Chicago, Illinois. The rehearsal dinner is the night before, place TBD. Start reserving your flights!

E-mail #3: Transportation
To: Groomsmen, Ushers
cc: The Bride
From: The Groom
Subject: Where to stay, where to play

We've blocked a series of rooms at the Swanky Hotel (312-555-5124) for our wedding guests. Mention my last name when booking, and try for one of the suites. It looks like United has the best rates right now, so don't delay!

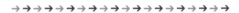

E-mail #4: What to Wear
To: Groomsmen, Ushers
cc: The Bride
From: The Groom
Subject: Dapper dudes

We've picked out some sweet-looking tuxes. Here's the deal.
Tuxedo style:
Brand/manufacturer:
Shirt style:
Tie:
Other accessories:
Attire can be rented from Penguin Suits, 111 Main Street, Chicago, (312) 555-1287. If you can't handle the task, e-mail my best man (and CC me) with your measure-ments.* It's coming down to the wire!

*See chapter 5 for more on measurements.

E-mail #5: Schedule of Events

To: Groomsmen, Ushers
cc: The Bride
From: The Groom
Subject: Where to be when

The day of the wedding we are meeting at 10:00 A.M. at the Swanky Hotel, 555 Michigan Ave., for some last-minute cheers and jeers. You'd better show up on time!

E-mail #6: Tuxedo Pickup Info

To: Groomsmen, Ushers
cc: The Bride
From: The Groom
Subject: Tux rental time

Tuxes will be ready for pickup on Wednesday, October 8 at Penguin Suits, 111 Main Street, (312) 555-1287. They close at six. Don't wait until the last minute!

→ → → → → → → → → → → → → → → → → → → →

THE VIRTUAL GROOM: Hit the Web to set up a listserv for your wedding party. If they don't already know one another, introduce your groomsmen and keep them in the loop with a listserv. It's a great way to keep them informed regarding attire, the bachelor party, hotel accommodations, and general guy stuff. Either create an e-mail string from which to "reply all," or head to Yahoo! Groups and set up a formal listserv.

→ → → **BONDING ON THE BIG DAY**

If your wedding doesn't start until nightfall, consider spending some last-minute guy time with your fellows. While your bride is off doing girly things with her attendants, plan a diverting activity, such as the following:

→ Golf, if time allows (you can't be on the seventh hole at 1:00 P.M. if the photographer is arriving at 2:00).

→ Play touch football, and then head to the pub for burgers and (a little) beer.

→ Eat a hearty breakfast at your favorite diner and trade war stories from your single days.

→ If you've never been a tourist in your own city, gather the troops for some sightseeing.

→ Organize a 5K "Race for the Groom" through the park. They'll let you win.

→ Grab a deck of cards and start dealing.

Let's face it—when it comes to weddings, some guys can be pretty unreliable. Here's what to do when a groomsman makes one of the following blunders:

✳ **He doesn't send measurements.**

Measurements should be taken and tuxes reserved at least three months in advance. If one of your guys hasn't fed you his info, call him up or e-mail him with a little reminder. If daily notification doesn't work, pick a pit bull (one of your more responsible groomsmen) to call him up and get the job done.

✳ **He doesn't make travel arrangements.**

Go online, find flight options, and e-mail him an itinerary with a note saying that you've noticed prices going up in the last couple of days (little white lies can come in handy). Place a room on hold under his name and tell him he has twenty-four hours to call up with his credit card info before all rooms are booked. Or bring in the pit bull to get the job done.

✳ **He's chronically late.**

Always tell him an earlier start time, like thirty minutes before you really need him to be there. Keep all the other groomsmen in on the game.

✳ **He disses the bride.**

If you hear that a groomsman is talking smack about your sweetie, speak up—you gotta be the pit bull here. Tell him you've heard through the grapevine that he's been saying some negative things about your fiancée. Maybe he's jealous of all the attention you're getting and a heart-to-heart might be just the thing to smooth things over. If it's more serious, you should decide together whether his role as a groomsman is the right fit.

Your best bet? Avoid the trenches and have your best man handle it. Well, everything but defending your bride's honor—that's your job.

Groomsmen Gifts

GIFTS FOR YOUR GUYS

We've talked about what they will do for you. Now, what will you do for them? That you totally appreciate your wedding party goes without saying, but tradition dictates that you show your gratitude by picking up some gifts. Every guy gets one: best man, groomsmen, ushers, even your ring bearer. Are all gifts the same? Not quite. The best man usually gets a little something extra, ushers get something modest, and kids get something age appropriate.

GIFT DISBURSEMENT ETIQUETTE

The rehearsal dinner is traditionally a great time to dole out the loot. Wrap each present individually with a nice note attached, and leave it at the recipient's place setting or stage a dramatic public giving. If you feel awkward about giving presents to a select few in front of onlookers, consider another time, like the actual rehearsal, after the dinner over a drink, or on the wedding morning as you are all getting dressed.

What to Give

Conflicted about how much to spend? This is really up to you, but remember: you'll never feel bad for being too generous, but you will if you're too cheap. Consider what they're spending for your wedding (engagement party gifts, formalwear rental, bachelor party) and try to return the favor. You can't go wrong with monogrammed or personalized items, but here are some other great gift ideas to get you on your way:

- Watches
- Swiss Army knives
- Coordinating wedding ties or cuff links
- Personalized golf balls
- Sunglasses
- Golf clubs
- Bar sets
- Gift certificates to a steakhouse
- Concert tickets
- Video games
- Palm Pilots
- Monogrammed money clips
- MP3 players
- Poker chip sets
- Tuxedo rentals for the wedding
- Gym bags
- CDs (or credit for music downloads)

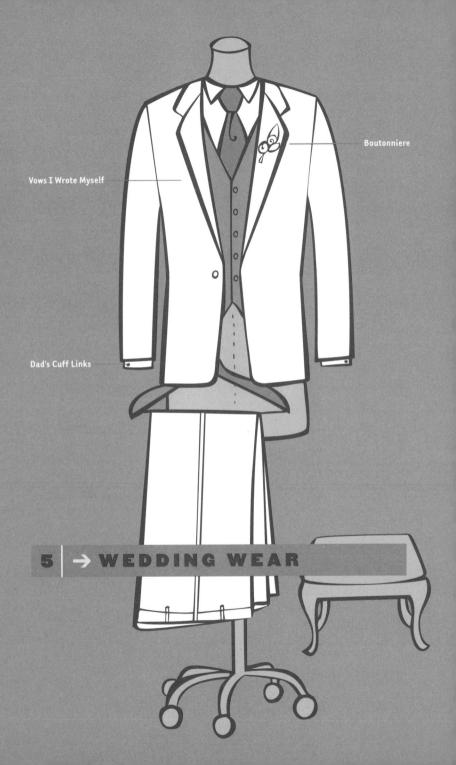

Boutonniere

Vows I Wrote Myself

Dad's Cuff Links

5 → WEDDING WEAR

ON your wedding day, you can't just show up in any old tuxedo. You'll want to look as stylish as you possibly can—and that takes some planning. Your wedding attire should fit the time of day and formality of the event. Tradition has dictated that afternoon ceremonies require one tuxedo style while evening affairs require another. Nowadays, dress codes aren't as strict but it's still helpful to use them as a guide.

About three months before the wedding, start firming up your look. You can certainly decide on your wedding wear before then, but your style selections should be in place no later than six weeks before you walk down that aisle. Once you've figured out what you want to wear, gather up all those guys you've enlisted to be by your side, take their measurements, and check out how they look in the chosen duds. In this chapter, we help you get it all done with a complete head-to-toe guide on looking fine. We'll cover everything from what to wear when and how to tie a bow tie to purchasing a wedding ring. We'll give you a glossary of tuxedo terms and essential grooming tips. When you're done, you'll certainly be one dapper groom.

WHAT TO WEAR WHEN

Your attire needs to reflect the occasion. Sure it's a wedding, but different types of events call for different pieces of formalwear. You wouldn't wear snow boots to the beach (unless you were severely misguided), and you wouldn't sport a stroller coat if your wedding was taking place at sunset in Jamaica. The setting, time, and formality of the day will all factor into your look. Check out our detailed chart on the facing page for what's hot when.

JACKETS

Tuxedo/Stroller

Double-Breasted Tuxedo

Mandarin

Full Dress Tailcoat

Cutaway

The Mood	Your Attire
Ultraformal daytime	To go ultraformal during the day, pick a cutaway coat, gray-striped trousers, gray vest, ascot, and black shoes. Adding the top hat, spats, and gray gloves are your call, governor. *The look: Prince Charles*
Formal daytime	Tux, tails, strollers—they all work. A black or gray morning coat with black or gray trousers would be flawless. Match the jacket with a white spread-collar shirt, a vest to match your coat, an ascot or standard necktie, plus a pocket square if you want to be extra dapper. *The look: Hugh Grant*
Semiformal daytime	Tweak some of the rules for this event. Try a black tux or a dark suit with a tone-on-tone shirt set (translation: using two colors from the same family, like a gray shirt and a long platinum tie). Anything blue, green, or even purple would work too. Summer grooms get a break: a light-colored suit and a white shirt—with or without a tie—will suffice. *The look: Marc Anthony*
Dressy casual daytime	It may not feel groomish, but white pants and a blue blazer will do—especially if you're getting married near the water. Or kick it up a notch and opt for a full khaki or linen suit with a light-colored shirt and optional tie. You can get away with a navy blue suit, but if you do anything dressier, the casual tone of the affair is lost. Get this: leather sandals or flip-flops are acceptable! *The look: Ralph Lauren*
Ultraformal evening	For evening, usher in the white tie. Do a black tailcoat, black trousers, white piqué wing-collared shirt, black vest or cummerbund, and white bow tie. *The look: James Bond*
Formal evening	What's called for is the classic groom ensemble: a black tux, white wing- or spread-collar shirt, black vest or cummerbund, and black bow tie. Lots of guys are now ditching the bow for a formal long tie—a contemporary option for the fashion-forward groom. If you're getting hitched in the summer, an appropriate look is a white dinner jacket with formal trousers. *The look: Rat Pack*
Semiformal evening	Take one classic tux ensemble but switch out the bow tie and call in the long silk tie. A solid-color tie in black, champagne, or gold will really keep the look evening appropriate. The alternative: a nice dark suit. In that case, the shirt should be white with a turned-down collar. The white dinner jacket works for summer or tropical destination weddings. (In any other scenario you might look like a waiter.) *The look: Brad Pitt*
Dressy casual evening	Skip the tux. Choose a solid-colored suit, maybe navy or charcoal, a white shirt, and a graphic tie. You could grab a workday tie from your closet (avoiding the one with the Playboy bunny logo), but you really should splurge on a new piece of wedding neckwear. The print should coordinate with the wedding colors—or at least not clash. *The look: Matthew Broderick*

Why buy: Buying a decent tux will run you $250 to $800, and a designer tux can cost as much as $1,600. If you get invited to a lot of functions (work or play) a tux is a good investment—it'll pay for itself after three or four events. And as long as you don't overindulge in good eats and you stick with a classic black tuxedo with a notched or shawl collar, you can wear it for years.

Why rent: If you don't attend many formal events or your weight is constantly in flux, renting is probably the way to go. The cost is 25 percent of buying new. Renting also lets you get something stylish or trendy without worrying that those extra-wide lapels will be passé next year.

LAPELS

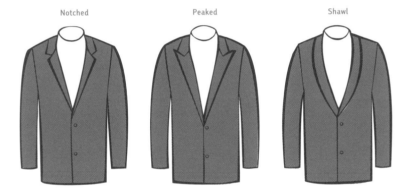

Notched   Peaked   Shawl

THE GROOM'S COMPANION

If you're renting a tux, you'll choose it based on the jacket, and wear whichever pants come with it. While you may get to make basic choices (pleated or flat front), don't expect to dictate the exact width of that little satin stripe down the seam. Here's a quick education on the world of wedding wear.

Note: There are always more contemporary fashion options available, but since styles are always changing we decided to stick with the basics. If you want to go for a trendier look in color, collar style, or length (standard tux jackets measure 32 inches but longer styles are currently in vogue), think of how it'll look in pictures ten years from now. (Those powder-blue tuxes used to be so cool!)

Jackets

Jackets are pretty much a wedding must, but you have many styles and colors (white or black, dark gray or light gray) to choose from.

Tuxedo: The tux can be single breasted (with a one- to four-button front) or double breasted (with a two- to six-button front).

Stroller coat: This semiformal suit jacket is cut like a tux but can be charcoal gray or black.

Full dress: Known as tails or a tailcoat. It actually has tails, with a two- to six-button front.

Cutaway: The morning coat, as it is also known, is short in front and long in back and tapers from the front waist button to a wide back tail. It's usually gray or black and paired with matching striped pants. Only worn at formal daytime affairs.

Mandarin: The good old Nehru jacket, or Mao, has a stand-up collar with no lapel and must be worn with a Mandarin-collar shirt. This combo does not require a tie. Score!

Lapels

History shows that lapels are subject to change (remember those wide ones in the '70s?). You'll want to stay current.

Notched: This baby features a triangular indentation where the lapel joins the collar and is the least formal of all styles.

Peaked: What you get here is a broad, V-shaped lapel that points up and out just below the collar line.

Shawl: A smooth, rounded lapel with no notch.

Shirts

When choosing a shirt, pay special attention to the quality of the cotton. Fine cotton will look dressier than cotton weaves and other fabrics, and will also feel supremely comfortable against your skin. Then, there are other decisions you need to make.

Piqué shirt: The standard stiff-fronted shirt has a central front panel made of piqué–a thick cotton fabric with a dimpled surface.

Plain front: A dress shirt without pleats in front. They come with buttons or holes for studs (hint: studs are more traditional for tuxedos).

Pleated front: A dress shirt with pleats–it's really a style preference.

French cuffs: Foldover cuffs with holes for cuff links, French cuffs must be worn with cuff links or cuff knots (colored fabric knots that hold the cuff together).

Barrel cuffs: Cuffs secured with one or more buttons.

Collars

At the end of the day, what really matters is the part you see . . . the collar. This is what separates a good shirt from a basic button-down. Your collar should flatter the shape of your face; luckily, you have lots of options.

Turndown collar: Also called a laydown collar, it's a tuxedo shirt with a regular collar and pleated front. Similar to a business shirt collar.

Wing collar: The most formal choice and the one most often worn with a tuxedo jacket. It stands up and has downward points.

Spread collar: This one resembles the standard button-front shirt but folds over and around the neck, with a wide division between points in front. The wider collar makes a good choice with a Euro tie (see page 101) or a standard necktie with a Windsor tie-knot.

Crosswyck: Sounds like a virus, but this collar crosses in the front and is fastened with a shiny button.

Banded collar: Also called a Mandarin collar. Both terms refer to a collar that stands up around the neck, above the tux buttons.

Turndown   Wing   Spread   Crosswyck   Banded

SHOPPING SMARTS

Once you've selected a style, you have to actually go and see how it looks.

Where to Go

Know that all tuxedo stores are not the same. Don't just choose a company based on its convenient location. Look for one with the best selection, best service, and best knowledge. Ask for recommendations from former grooms and groomsmen for a top-quality store that will show you countless tuxedo styles as well as shirts, ties, cuff links, cummerbunds, and shoes to complete the look. If you're surrounded by bachelors (or you don't trust your married pals) search the Web for potential shops to check out. Call ahead and ask about the range of tuxedos they have. Narrow down your list and hit the stores.

Be a Spy Guy

The second you walk into a place, you'll be able to suss out the overall vibe. How busy is the shop and how attentive are the salespeople? Start to inquire about specifics like rental policies, pickup times, and group discounts. Are there other grooms in the store? Subtly eavesdrop on their interactions—do the salespeople seem to have a helpful and professional attitude?

Call in the Troops

Once you've found a terrific tuxedo shop to dress you to the nines, make a date there with your best man and one or two groomsmen to get measured and start trying on styles. Comfort is crucial. You need to move without difficulty. Audition the outfit by shaking your groove thing in the dressing room (make sure the door is locked). You'll be twisting and turning in this getup for eight or more hours, so you'll want to feel at ease. That said, it's not a sweat suit, so don't expect complete coziness.

If the Suit Fits

Whether you're renting or buying, most shops will custom fit your purchase (that's why you need to start the process early—to allow for alterations). No matter which tuxedo style you choose, a few basic fit rules apply:

- The jacket sleeve hem should fall at your wrist bone.
- The bottom hem of your jacket should cover your butt and the vent shouldn't pull open. If it does, that means it's too tight.
- The jacket should hug your shoulders perfectly—if it's too big it could create a fold of fabric down your spine.

- The collar should lie flat on the back and sides of your neck without any gaps or bulges.
- About $1/4$ to $1/2$ inch of your shirt cuff should show below the jacket sleeve.
- Flat-front pants are generally more slimming than their pleated counterpart—less fabric gives the illusion of less weight.
- Your pants should break across the top of your shoes.

Time with the Tux

If you're renting, your tuxedo should be ready for pickup three days before the wedding. Try it on right away to check the fit and make sure it's the right tux (you don't want to surprise your bride with a navy-blue ensemble). Since most rentals must be returned to the store the day after the event, make a plan with your best man to take it back for you.

ACCESSORY ESSENTIALS

Your tuxedo can't very well stand on its own. Here's a secret every woman knows: accessories add personality to a traditional look. To take advantage of her fashion smarts, keep your fiancée in on the equation.

If she's adamant that you not wear something in particular (like an orange-and-blue bow tie), she's probably saving you from looking like a fool.

Ties

Classic bow ties are great. They are usually black but can be white for a superformal affair. Colors are also a good choice if you want to show some spice or match the wedding party. (We're sure that you weren't thinking chartreuse—and that you don't even know what that color looks like.) But depending on your jacket, a host of other options await:

Necktie: A standard tie, in formal black or a subtle pattern.

Ascot: Wide, formal ascot ties are usually patterned as well, worn folded over and fastened with a stickpin or tie tack. They're for ultraformal daytime weddings and are worn with a cutaway coat and striped gray trousers.

Bolo: If you're having a Western-themed wedding, live in Santa Fe, or really love John Wayne, try a bolo tie, which usually has a silver or turquoise design at the throat.

THE VIRTUAL GROOM: Hit the Web to find local tux rental locations and view formalwear options. Do your groomsmen live all over the country? Search online for a company with a store in each guy's area and in the town in which you're going to marry.

Euro tie: A hybrid between an ascot and a regular old necktie. The look? A long, square-bottom tie knotted at the neck and worn with a wing- or spread-collar shirt.

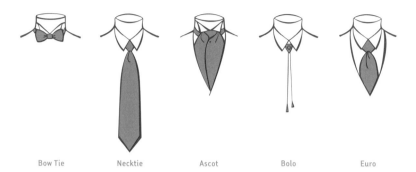

| Bow Tie | Necktie | Ascot | Bolo | Euro |

Cuff Links

Cuff links can make or break an outfit. Be outlandish with mini Scrabble tiles on your wrists or stick with simple elegance: black with a gold outline. A lot of grooms receive a special pair from their brides as a gift on the big day; know that you'll be required to wear these no matter what. Pocket squares and funky suspenders are other ways to inject a little life into your ensemble.

Cummerbunds

A cummerbund is a band of pleated fabric worn around the waist. To avoid wearing it

upside down—a common blunder—think of old-fashioned Broadway theatergoers, who placed tickets in their cummerbunds, to help you remember that the pleats go upward. Never worn with a belt, the cummerbund is usually basic black but you (or your bride) might want a color to match the bridesmaids' dresses or flowers. For an ultraformal evening wedding, a white tie and cummerbund rocks.

Boutonniere

Though your tux is sure to turn heads, your boutonniere will also be front and (off) center throughout the day. You don't want to feel awkward in a frilly flower with iri-descent ribbons. Check out classic blooms you'd feel comfortable sporting, like lily of the valley or a red rose.

Shoes

When it comes to your feet, the traditional look is formal black patent-leather shoes. If you're just not down with the shine, look for matte-finish formal leather shoes or fun wingtip shoes. If you don't own your own, black rental shoes are essential. The biggest possible fashion faux pas? Brown shoes or sloppy old black ones. And remember to match your socks to your pants (which should match your shoes).

→ → → **HOW TO TIE A BOW TIE**

There's no reason to wear one of those ready-made bow ties when tying the perfect bow is an easy six-step process. It's just like tying your shoe:

1 Put the tie around your neck so that end A (on your left) is longer than end B.
2 Cross end A over the top of B.
3 Pull end A up and behind end B.
4 Create a loop (and half of the bow) with end B.
5 Bring A to hang in front of the loop you just formed.
6 Hold everything in place, pulling end A behind the tie from below, then folding it in half to create the other side of the bow. Poke this loop through the space behind loop B.

Done! (If it looks bedraggled, adjust the tie by tugging at its ends and straightening the center knot. If it looks awful, try it again.)

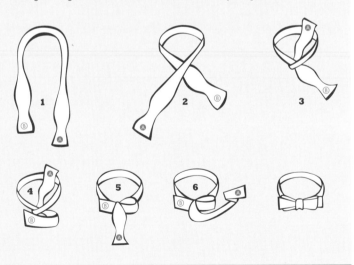

DRESSING THE GUYS

Once you and your main squeeze have solidified your look, decide on a similar, if not identical, look for your wedding party. If all or most of the men in your group own tuxes, they can wear what they have, but be specific about the shirt and accessories they need to wear. In this situation, the groom will usually buy all the guys a smart-looking tie to wear at the wedding.

GETTING THE GROOMSMEN'S GOODS

If they'll all be renting, you should organize a group outing at your preferred tuxedo shop about three months before the wedding (lure them with the promise of brews afterward). If you run into scheduling conflicts, tell those who can't make it to provide you with their exact measurements. And this is not a guessing game. Make sure they hit up a local tuxedo shop or professional tailor to get the right measurements (inseam, sleeve length, and so on–see page 104 for the specifics). Then reserve all the tuxedos to be picked up and tested out when everyone assembles a couple of days before the big day. Even though you and the best man will coordinate this effort, breathe a sigh of budget relief, because the guys will pay for their own tuxedos.

YOUR DAD'S WEAR

The dads should also be a part of this process. Their respective tuxedos don't need to perfectly match the groomsmen but they should certainly fit the formality of the event. The only exceptions are boys under six; tuxedos aren't necessary (and may not be available) for little tykes.

Make sure your out-of-town guys have all the right specs with this fill-in-the-blank size card. Xerox it for them; or for you techies: scan this page, save as a PDF, and e-mail it to your guys.

Name: _____

Address: _____

Phone: _____

E-mail: _____

Groom's Name: _____

Bride's Name: _____

Wedding Date: _____

Coat: _____

Chest: _____

Overarm: _____

Shirt neck: _____

Shirt sleeve: _____

Pant waist: _____

Pant inseam: _____

Pant outseam: _____

Hip: _____

Shoe size: _____

Height: _____

Weight: _____

STAND OUT FROM THE CROWD

If all the guys wear tuxes, you'll want some detail that differentiates you from the rest of the pack. You are the groom, after all. Try these ideas on for size.

You wear . . .

- A tailcoat while groomsmen sport standard tuxes.
- A white dinner jacket while the men stick with black.
- A silver or white vest while the groomsmen's vest color coordinates with that of the bridesmaids' dresses.
- A different tie to complement the bride's gown. You can even get a tie made from the extra fabric left over from her wedding gown.
- A white bow tie while the guys wear standard black ones.
- A military uniform (if applicable).
- A pocket square instead of a boutonniere.
- A different boutonniere (read on for cool flowers to latch onto your lapel).

→ → → A BANGING BOUTONNIERE

Give your suit (or tux) some personality with a signature stem

- → Pair a single rose with rosemary and seeded eucalyptus for a clean, classic look with a touch of texture.

- → Go for a flirtier look (yes, even on a guy) with a few sprigs of hydrangea in a fun color, such as lime green.

- → Pair a dark flower with bright, fresh greenery (like a Black Magic rose on a bed of lady's mantle) for a striking but sophisticated contrast.

- → Go mod or minimal—we love the look of a single white cymbidium orchid.

- → Forgo flowers altogether and choose unripened berries—perfect for a summer or fall wedding, one taking place at a vineyard, or a wedding where fruit will play a recurring role in other elements of the wedding day (the invitations, the wedding cake, and the table centerpieces).

GROOM GROOMING TIPS

We know you're planning on getting a haircut, but remember you'll be the subject of countless photos that will capture your look for the rest of your life. You need to make sure you take extra care of your appearance for your wedding day—at least for your bride's sake. We're not talking about months of beauty boot camp. Just a few little things that will help you shine—in the good sense.

Two months or more before:

We could all stand to lose a few pounds, but it may not be a bad idea to make a special effort to exercise and eat right starting at least two months before the wedding. You'll look and feel better, guaranteed (remember, the camera adds ten pounds!).

One week before:

Now about that haircut: schedule it for one week before your wedding to avoid that just-trimmed look.

The day before:

Get yourself a manicure. Don't be scared: they don't polish your nails—they just trim them evenly, cut off those ragged cuticles, and buff them like a car. You'll be shaking hundreds of hands, and neatly trimmed nails will make a good impression.

The big day:

Don't be surprised if your bride suggests that you dust your forehead with a little powder (as long as she isn't suggesting eyeliner, we promise you she has your best interests in mind). Translucent powder reduces shine so you won't look like a grease ball in wedding photos. Consider a return visit to the barber the morning of the big day for a professional, lathered-up shave. If you are the five-o'clock shadow type and your wedding is in the evening, hold off until the afternoon to shave. With that, combined with fresh breath and a splash (really, just a splash) of cologne, you'll be ready to amaze her at the altar.

Here are some solutions to your most pressing grooming problems:

- Shaving bumps: Shave with the grain (not against it) in the spots where you get irritated. Use a lubricating shave gel (not foam) on wet skin, and let it soak in for a few minutes to straighten the follicle. Then shave with a man-ual–not electric–blade. Keep this up and you'll see fewer bumps in about six weeks.

- Unibrow: The best way to handle out-of-control eyebrows is to wax, if you can be a man and handle a little pain. Waxed hairs will take longer to grow back and, when they eventually do, they will grow in thinner and more sparsely. If pain isn't your game, ask your barber to trim your brows with scissors (which will at least keep you from looking like you have bangs). Whatever you do, don't shave your brows–you'll be asking for unsightly stubble and potential ingrown hairs.

- Breakout from hell: If your acne feeds on pressure, you may need to ward off an attack a week in advance by taking a prescription steroid (check with your doctor). If it's too late and a monster has already arrived, a dermatol-ogist can give you a cortisone cream to immediately reduce swelling and redness. Can't get to a doctor? An over-the-counter topical cream with sul-fur will dry out a bad spot–ask the pharmacist for such a blemish buster.

- Excessive sweating: Technically called *hyperhidrosis*, this overabundance of perspiration in your armpits and palms is often triggered by stressful sit-uations (getting married might be considered stressful). When over-the-counter products don't work, you might need to ask your doctor about a serious prescription antiperspirant.

THE WEDDING RINGS

I t's the most important accessory of the day. Buying your bands is something you'll do together about four months before the big day, allowing time for engraving. But there's nothing traditional about men's wedding rings today. (Translation: they do not look like heavy gold lug nuts.)

ROOM FOR THE GROOM

One of the first-time ring wearer's biggest complaints is pinched skin. Rings are now available in a "comfort fit," where the interior is curved, not flat, so digits won't fidget for space. Jewelers even make ergonomic rings designed so that the plain, tapered bottoms absorb the brunt of abuse while the showier top half stays relatively unscathed.

MARRIAGE MATERIALS

From most to least expensive, your metal choices are platinum, white or yellow gold, and even sterling silver. According to jewelers, the matte finish is highly popular right now, but keep in mind that with this finish scratches can quickly mar its appearance, requiring some maintenance.

FLASHY FINGERS

Remember, you're not shopping for a Super Bowl ring—and chances are you don't need to sport a lot of bling in your field. Stones are usually set to be flush with the surface of the ring to create a smooth, secure exterior. Many hip styles incorporate gypsy- and channel-set round or square diamonds. And you can choose classic ice or get funky with black, champagne, or yellow diamonds.

With two to three months left, you'll want to send your band out to be engraved. Although a nickname, promise, date, or saying that bears significance to you two alone may be ideal (the interiors of one celeb couple's rings read "A deal's a deal"), here are some inscriptions with timeless appeal:

Semper amemus (Latin: "Let us love always")

Amor vincit omnia (Latin: "Love conquers all")

Mizpah (Hebrew, Genesis 31:48-49: "God will watch over us when we are apart")

Amore mio (Italian: "My love")

Por tous jours (fifteenth-century French: "For all the days")

Mon coeur est a vous (French: "You have my heart")

Par grant amour (fourteenth- or fifteenth-century French: "For my greatest love")

Je t'aime (French: "I love you")

Myn genyst (Old German: "My heart")

Forever

Always and forever

Love is eternal

Never to part

More than words can say

6 → THE CEREMONY

The Game Plan

CEREMONIES are in dire need of an image makeover. The most important part of the wedding day (after all, this is when you will formally proclaim your commitment to your lady), the ceremony is considered by many grooms to be a standard, one-size-fits-all affair. It often gets overlooked in the planning of the more-boisterous reception. But really, your ceremony should be the most personal part of the day. It should fit the wedding mood, and your vows should be given as much weight as your cake. Depending on the type of service you and your fiancée choose to have (religious or civil), you may be limited to a set structure. But there's no reason you can't add a dose of you to the mix.

In this chapter we give you the goods on everything ceremony related—from where to have it to how to choose your officiant. We'll break down the specifics of who stands where and what should happen when. And we'll give you ideas for how to personalize your day with vows straight from the heart.

WHERE TO BEGIN

Early on in the planning (while you're envisioning the event), sit down with your fiancée and discuss what kind of ceremony you want.

SERVICE STYLES

The most prevalent types are religious, interfaith, and civil. Whether you want the traditional marriage ritual in your childhood synagogue or a quickie secular ceremony performed by a judge, your ceremony should be a reflection of you. If both of you are from the same religious and social backgrounds this should be a fairly easy decision. But interfaith ceremonies are now more common and not the difficult rituals to plan that they once were.

WHERE TO WALK THE AISLE

You'll need to decide on a location for your service once you've answered the big question, religious or secular? Your choice may fall easily into place—a Catholic ceremony must be held in a Catholic church to be recognized as official. But other faiths can be more lenient on this point and, if you don't feel tied to your place of worship (or if your families aren't pressuring you to marry there), the possibilities are endless: in a garden or vineyard, on the beach, on a boat. From a convenience standpoint, it may make the most sense to hold the ceremony at the reception site if space allows. Most places accustomed to weddings will know how to set up the ceremony, perhaps using a portion of the reception room. Of course, a Vegas-type chapel or city hall is always an option—even when you have time on your side.

CHOOSING YOUR OFFICIANT

You may have already solved this one when you settled on a ceremony location. A religious ceremony in a house of worship usually comes as a nice, neat package, complete with officiant. Sometimes your ceremony site will have a hands-off approach, allowing you to use their structure but requiring you to bring in your own priest or rabbi. If you're exchanging vows elsewhere and don't have a family priest or rabbi who's known you since birth, you'll need to find someone to marry you. Here's how:

- Ask around. Find out who performed the services for married friends and family members.
- Go online. Local resources with lists of officiants are available at many wedding Web sites.
- Call your county clerk's office. If you'll go the civil route, call your local government and find out who performs wedding ceremonies.
- Pick a friend. These days, laymen can be ordained via the Internet and actually receive the power to marry you. Maybe someone you and your finacée deem too special to be relegated to the regular wedding party would love to have the honor of pronouncing you husband and wife. But make sure he knows what he's getting into.

THE VIRTUAL GROOM: Hit the Web to ordain your officiant. If your brother or your uncle offers to marry you, feel free to take him up on that. There are several Web sites where you can have your favorite person granted legal permission to perform wedding ceremonies. But make sure he's not a jokester.

Interview Clues

When you meet with a potential officiant, you should discuss your wedding plans, find out if the officiant is open to your ideas, and decide if the three of you want to work together. You should be comfortable with this person and appreciate his or her style—he or she will be marrying you, after all. Don't forget to do the following:

- Ask about any rules or requirements (such as certain ceremony times or restrictions on aisle runners).
- Find out if any pre-wedding counseling is required.
- Determine if the officiant will give a sermon or a speech.
- Inquire about the fee—we're not going to let you break that budget!

Traditionally it's the groom's responsibility to pay for and organize the securing of the marriage license, so you'll need to do some research on the matter.

When: Most marriage licenses are valid only for a short amount of time–typically, you must marry within a month or two of applying for the license.

Where: Every state has its own set of rules, so you'll have to find out exactly what you need to do for the state you're marrying in. Hear that? You must get a marriage license in the state where you will be exchanging vows, not where you currently live. Call the county clerk's office for the location in which your ceremony will be held to find out all the details, like hours of operation and expiration dates.

What you need: Ask what specific documents are necessary. Many wedding Web sites (like www.TheKnot.com) list marriage requirements for all states, but it's always a good idea to follow up with the county office to make sure the rules haven't changed. You don't want to find out after all these months of hard work that your marriage isn't legal!

Here's what some of the regulations cover:

→ Legal age

→ Blood test requirements

→ Residency requirements

→ Fee

→ ID

→ Who must be present to apply

→ Who signs

→ Waiting period

→ Valid period

PERSONALIZING YOUR CEREMONY

I n this era of banishing the cookie-cutter wedding, you may want to incorporate elements in your ceremony that express your personalities. Officiant permitting, you might walk down the aisle to your favorite rock song, ask your father to read a passage from a humor book, or sound the bells once you've sealed your marriage with a kiss.

THE SOUND OF MUSIC

As with all ceremony details, first check with your officiant or site manager to find out about music regulations. For example, some Catholic priests and Jewish rabbis will not allow Wagner's "Bridal Chorus" ("Here Comes the Bride")–the priests because it's a secular work (some Catholic parishes do not allow secular music at all), and the rabbis because of Wagner's well-documented anti-Semitism. So if you have plans for pop tunes or even Pachelbel, clear up potential issues beforehand. Your officiant should be able to recommend suitable substitutes.

Song Spots

Most wedding ceremonies, civil or religious, call for music in at least three places: before the wedding (the prelude), during the processional, and during the recessional. You may also include post-ceremony music (the postlude) and/or additional songs–interludes–during the ceremony (perhaps a deceased relative's favorite piece).

The Prelude: Starting as soon as the doors open, this music is intended to entertain guests as they enter, are seated, and wait for the ceremony to begin. Preludes establish the mood. Factor in traffic problems, tardy VIPs, and other unforeseen delays, and plan thirty to forty-five minutes of music in case you have to start the ceremony a couple minutes late. A solo flutist, violinist, or pianist is a low-key choice.

The Processional: Processional music plays as the bride and her wedding party make their grand entrance. For this reason, it's usually associated with wedding drama and pageantry—few can resist featuring the richest, most rousing musical accompaniments. Many couples opt for the grandeur of Mozart's "Wedding March" or the soothing power of Pachelbel's Canon in D, but any music (or instrument) will do, so long as it strikes an emotionally charged chord.

The Recessional: Despite the pomp and circumstance of the processional, recessional music is hardly an afterthought. You can make your exit as dramatic and flamboyant as you want, but remember that recessional music is usually joyful or festive (think Beethoven's "Ode to Joy" or Stevie Wonder's "Signed, Sealed, Delivered"). Choose something that will complement your giddy, glowing demeanor and pump up the crowd for your reception.

READ UP ON READINGS

Ask friends, relatives, parents, stepparents, or mentors to read during your ceremony. You might choose several long readings and have just a few readers, or select five or six short passages and include more in the party. You and your honey can also read alternating verses of a poem or different prose passages. Print your readers' names and the selections they'll perform in your wedding program. And make several copies of the readings and ask the best man to hold on to them, in case anyone forgets to bring his or her own.

Ceremony Speak

Don't know where to start looking for readings? Depending on your ceremony type, you may be limited to religious text. The Bible is rich with classic passages—your officiant can point you in the right direction. If you're having a nondenominational ceremony, feel free to pick unorthodox passages—prose or poems you both love or whose sentiments mean something to you. Shakespeare, Lawrence Ferlinghetti, a book of love letters (from writer James Joyce to his wife, Nora, for example), *The Giving Tree*—these are a few good places to find some words from the heart. In the end, if you just aren't finding anything that speaks to you, look to your readers for help—maybe they've already come across the perfect reading for your wedding. Or you could send them on the literary hunt. If it's a passage they feel passionate about, your ceremony will be that much more personal.

YOUR STEP-BY-STEP CEREMONY

The wedding rituals for your ceremony will differ based on your religious and personal preferences, so look to your chosen officiant for the specifics of the day, either weeks ahead or the night before at the rehearsal. Don't take the rehearsal lightly. You'll want to look (and feel) like you know what you're doing on this incredibly important day.

Step 1: Separate the Sea

As the doors open, your well-chosen ushers will lead guests to their seats. In traditional Christian ceremonies, the bride's side is the left side of the church when looking from back to front and the groom's side is the right; for Jewish services, it's the opposite. However, this segregation doesn't have to be strictly enforced. If one side of the family will have more guests than the other, ushers should try to even things out.

Step 2: Save Seats

The first four or five rows should be reserved for immediate and extended family. Immediate family members are seated just before the ceremony begins. Your siblings (if not in the wedding party) are seated earlier than grandparents and great-grandparents. Siblings sit either in the first row with parents or in the second row with grandparents.

Step 3: Take a Walk

In Christian traditions you take your place at the altar flanked by the officiant and your best man before your parents take their turn down the aisle. In the Jewish faith, you follow the best man to the altar, escorting both your parents down the aisle. The bride's mother is *always* seated last at a Christian ceremony; your mother is seated with your father just before the bride's mother takes her seat. The seating of the bride's mother signals that the ceremony is about to begin. (In Jewish ceremonies, parents stand under the chuppah with the couple.)

Step 4: Listen Up

What happens from here will vary, but in general your ceremony will include some of the following elements: opening words, opening prayers, declaration of consent (where you say you're not being forced into marrying your fiancée), presentation of the bride (to you!), and the readings.

Step 5: Say I Do

After all the readings, it's time to exchange vows. Either the officiant will guide you through traditional religious or secular vows, or you'll dazzle your darling with some words from the heart. (See page 120 for all your vow needs.)

CEREMONY PROCESSION ORDER

Christian

Bride and her escort | Flower Girl | Honor Attendant | Bridesmaid | Officiant | Groom | Best Man

Jewish

Bride and her parents | Honor Attendant | Bridesmaids | Groom and his parents | Best Man and Groomsmen | Grandparents of the Bride | Grandparents of the Groom | Rabbi and Cantor

Step 6: Ring True

The presentation of the rings seals the deal. The officiant will ask for them (make sure either you or the best man has them in a secure pocket!). As you exchange rings, you generally say "With this ring, I thee wed." Depending on your venue's restrictions, you may add something a bit more personal about what the ring and your lady mean to you.

Step 7: Kiss Her

This is the part of the ceremony everyone's been waiting for, so make it special. Don't feel strange about practicing beforehand—it's not every day that involves serious PDA (in front of friends and family, no less). Practice makes perfect. A peck will look cold and perfunctory, but visible tongue action is tacky and crass (don't forget that the first row of pews isn't far away). Strike a balance between the two, and do it until you feel comfortable enough to do it on command in front of your brand-new in-laws.

Step 8: Take a Breath

Your ceremony recessional will likely feel more fluid than the processional—after all, you'll be married and will (hopefully) feel much less nervous! In Christian traditions, the procession is reversed and the men in the wedding party escort the women down the aisle, led by you and your new wife. In the Jewish tradition, both sets of parents follow you and the bride, and then your bridal party makes its move. Next up: time to celebrate!

→ → → **WALK DOWN THE AISLE IN STYLE**

Tradition states that at the beginning of the ceremony you should head to the front of the site with your officiant or your parents, but there are other options too. You could do any of the following:

→ Escort the bride. This works nicely when her parents or another close family member won't be walking down the aisle with her.

→ Meet the bride halfway.

→ Escort the mother of the bride up the aisle in the first part of the processional to show your solidarity.

→ Escort your grandparents. They'll be so touched.

→ Choose a special song just for your entrance (if permissible).

VOWS 101

TRADITIONAL TONGUES

Each religious faith has nuptial traditions and practices–including standard wedding vows–that have been passed down through generations. Exact phrases vary slightly from place to place and among different clergy. In traditional Catholic ceremonies, the words are something like "I, ___, take you, ___, for my lawful wife/husband, to have and to hold from this day forward, for better, for worse, for richer, for poorer, in sickness and health, until death do us part." If you and your fiancée aren't comfortable with the phrasing "I now pronounce you man and wife," be sure to address this point immediately.

In a traditional Jewish wedding–Orthodox and sometimes Conservative–only the groom speaks his vows, which can be recited in both Hebrew and English. In Reform services, both you and your fiancée speak. The original vow is (in English transliteration) *"Haray at mekudeshet lee beh-taba'at zo keh-dat Moshe veh-Yisrael,"* which translates to "Behold, you are consecrated to me with this ring according to the laws of Moses and Israel."

WRITING YOUR OWN VOWS

She wants you to write your own vows, but you're more Spicoli than Shakespeare. The last thing you composed was a fantasy football roster. Even if you're fully on board about writing your own vows, the process can be intimidating. Get the go-ahead from your officiant (you need to ask permission before straying from the traditional) and then prepare to express your devotion in a way that will make your fiancée proud. Memorize your speech but also keep a copy of it on you–exchanging your vows can be nerve wracking, and you want to be prepared if your mind naturally blanks.

Step 1: Share Stories

There are two options: You can prepare words for both of you to repeat, or surprise each other with original material. Decide on one. Obviously you cannot do any of this without first taking your fiancée's pulse. Make sure you're on the same page regarding the tone and the message you want to send people about your relationship. Think about what marriage means to both of you. What do you envision for your future, and how should this be expressed in words?

Step 2: Get Touchy-Feely

Great vows are the real thing (NFL), not hackneyed (XFL). Avoid clichés and anything that sounds like a high school yearbook inscription. You're speaking to the woman of your dreams–and she's no standard lady. She deserves inspired words and you want to show that she is singular. Extol her ability to mesmerize you with her beauty. Gentle ribbing ("I love you even if you don't agree with me that The Beatles are the world's greatest band.") is acceptable.

Step 3: Go Back to the Basics

Even if you don't want to take the conventional route, it's a good idea to check out the customary vows for your faith and use them as a jumping-off point. There might be a phrase or two that you find relevant to your modern union. These words have endured for a reason: people believe in them.

Step 4: Pick Up Pop Culture

Many couples borrow from movies, poems, songs, and novels. Maybe *Dumb and Dumber* has something? Maybe not. Jot down phrases that capture your feelings. Quote them outright or weave them into your words.

Step 5: Pull It All Together

Now it's time to take all the pieces and create your actual vows. Using words like *respect, cherish, love, support,* and *promise* is always good. Vows are the most important element of the ceremony, but that doesn't mean they should go on and on. Pack a punch with clarity, sincerity, and brevity.

→ → → **MAD LIB VOWS FOR THE LAST-MINUTE GROOM**

My dearest [**bride's name**], when I first saw you I said, "[**exclamation**]!" Your eyes shine like [**flattering noun**]. In them I can see our future. You are the most [**romantic adjective**] woman I know. I love you more than you can imagine. I am honored you have chosen me as your [**meaningful noun**]. I promise to always [**verb**] and [**loving gesture**]. I want to always make you feel [**affirmative adjective**], just like you make me feel [**sappy adjective**]. We make a good team. When you cry I will [**manly verb**] you. And when you laugh I will [**goofy verb**]. You are my [**noun**]. I will love you [**an unending length of time**].

Fig. 101:
The Witty Toast

YOU have the 411 on vendors, groomsmen, and your vows. There are just a few more things you need to know as you make final preparations. This chapter covers what's expected of you on your wedding day. As with everything wedding, whether you choose to follow tradition is up to you. From the grand entrance to the big exit, we'll take you through the biggies one by one, along with reception essentials like dealing with guests and handling any last-minute emergencies. Then we'll give you some stellar advice on making a toast (yes, you need to salute your new *wife*–that term will take time to get used to), being a good host, and leaving the party in style. Guys, let it all out because this is the end!

SEVEN-DAY COUNTDOWN

The race is heating up. Stay on track with this last-minute checklist.

- Double check the honeymoon reservations.
- Pack your honeymoon bags—and make sure they have luggage tags with your name, address, and phone number.
- Pick up traveler's checks.
- Get a haircut.
- Give the officiant's payment to your best man.
- Pick up your tux and make sure your groomsmen have done the same.
- Confirm rehearsal time with your officiant.
- Confirm arrangements with the rehearsal-dinner spot.
- Finalize seating chart.
- Confirm the vendors your bride's put you in charge of.
- Pack your wedding-day essentials (toothbrush, shaving kit, cologne, mouthwash).
- Make sure Aunt Bertha gets picked up at the airport and that Uncle Greg is situated at the hotel bar with a fresh martini.
- Hand the programs over to the right person and demonstrate how they should be displayed (for example, in baskets, on a table, ribbons to the left).
- Steal moments alone with your bride-to-be.
- Deliver goodie bags to the hotel and check to see that they all contain three, not two, fresh-baked cookies.

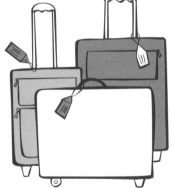

Luggage with Tags

THE NIGHT BEFORE

THE REHEARSAL DINNER

What: The purpose of this gathering is to toast and roast the couple on the eve of their wedding, have both families get acquainted, and dole out gifts to wedding attendants. Since this event is traditionally on your parents' list of things to do, it's a good idea to know what to expect (so you can share the info with them!). The rehearsal dinner is a good opportunity to add some personal flair—incorporate some menu items or decorations that just weren't appropriate for the main event. It *should* have a different feel from your wedding day—you never want to outshine that celebration.

Where: A local restaurant, family home, boat cruise—anywhere that holds your expected crowd. (See page 126 for more ideas.)

Who hosts: Make sure your parents know that this party is traditionally their responsibility—unless you've come to the decision that you and your bride will host the event, or that both sets of parents will share the duties. Ask your parents what they'd like to do and let your fiancée know. This can often be a tension-filled area for brides and grooms. Even if it's your parents' party, your fiancée may have her own ideas about the kind of party she thinks is best. You'll have to act as liaison between both women in your life (get used to it) and try to find a solution that makes everyone comfortable.

Who's invited: Aside from immediate family and the wedding-party members and their spouses, an invite is usually extended to out-of-town guests who will be arriving before the wedding day. Go over the list with your parents so you don't embarrass yourself by not remembering someone's name or history. These days, with three-day celebrations on the rise, it's not uncommon for everyone on the wedding guest list to be invited.

Groom's clues: As your family rep, you'll need to coordinate the guest lists, communicate about details with your fiancée and her family, and mediate any issues or conflicting expectations. You will need to schmooze a lot at this event—after all, you're hosting it with your parents. Be prepared to introduce your key family members to her key relatives. And be ready for a toast. Start with nice words about your bride, thank out-of-town guests, thank attendants on each side, raise your glass to your bride's family, and finally thank (and toast) your parents, who are most likely hosting this event.

Take the humdrum sit-down dinner to the next level with these six great ideas for a fun, festive fete!

Backyard barbecue. Bonding over burgers? Why not? A good old-fashioned cookout complete with red-and-white-checkered cloths is fun for the whole (extended) family. Save Dad from flipping burgers and look into hiring a grill master for the night.

Baseball game. Take them out to the ball game! Organize an outing to a local stadium for some hoots and hot dogs. Many ballparks offer group packages (a.k.a. budget relief) and even a congratulatory message on the scoreboard.

Global gathering. Get inspired by the world around you and host a Jamaican reggae bash with jerk chicken and steel drums, a Mexican fiesta with margaritas and piñatas, or a Moroccan merrymaking with couscous and belly dancers.

Wine tasting. Greet guests with some local libations at a nearby vineyard. A wine sampling with light bites (tasty apps) infuses a common cocktail party with a dash of class.

Clambake. A seafood shindig is shore to please (we had to say it) your coastal partygoers. Look for a catering company that specializes in clambakes, and remember to spread the word about the casual dress code.

Sushi soiree. Hire a sushi chef to make rolls to order (don't forget to offer teriyaki for those who don't do raw fish) and decorate with paper lanterns.

BEDTIME STORIES

One thing men often ask is whether they should spend the night before the wedding with their soon-to-be wives. The answer? Even if you've spent every night together for the last few years, we think it's a great idea to split up after the rehearsal dinner. Why? First, you'll be super excited (and super nervous), but you need a decent night's sleep. If the two of you stay up all night talking, there's no way that will happen.

Second, whether you see each other for the first time at a snap session or at the ceremony, you won't want to pass up the initial surprise of seeing each other all decked out in your tux and gown. Afraid you'll be too weirded out being on your own? Invite one of your sibs or a close friend to stay with you, or make it a party with all of your groomsmen (although this could be a recipe for disaster, so proceed with caution).

PRE-CEREMONY ANTICS

GETTING READY

One of the best things you can do on the day of your wedding is prepare a timeline to work from. Let's face it: most people, men and women, are nervous on the day of. Give yourself one less thing to stress over and go through the pre-wedding process with this checklist.

ITEMS TO REMEMBER

- ❏ Vows and toast
- ❏ Wedding rings (to hand to the best man before the ceremony)
- ❏ Tuxedo or suit
- ❏ Shirt
- ❏ Vest, cummerbund, or suspenders
- ❏ Studs or cuff links
- ❏ Tie
- ❏ Boxers or briefs
- ❏ Handkerchief
- ❏ Socks
- ❏ Shoes
- ❏ Comb

Alarm Clock

- ❏ Hair products
- ❏ Breath mints
- ❏ Toothpaste and toothbrush
- ❏ Shaving tools
- ❏ Deodorant
- ❏ Cologne (to be sparingly applied)
- ❏ Wallet (with plenty of cash)
- ❏ Any necessary prescriptions
- ❏ Pre- and post-party wear (for rehearsal dinner and brunch)

Wake Up on Time

When should you start getting ready? The timing of your affair makes all the difference here. Count backward from when you need to meet your bride. If it's a five-o'clock ceremony, be at the church at least an hour before that if you're taking pictures first; half an hour if you're not. Think about waking up around eight hours before (for a five-o'clock ceremony that means nine in the morning—see how easy it can be?). Take a minute to relish the momentous day that lies ahead. Then take a shower. Confirm that you have all the accessories you need—from boxers to breath mints. Eat a filling breakfast but don't test your heartburn tendency with new foods. (Oatmeal and bananas, yes. Huevos rancheros, maybe not.)

Get Organized

With around two hours of morning prep time (by eleven in the morning in our example), you should be ready to take care of all of the last-minute details that have been assigned to you (confirming cars, being there for the cake's delivery, what have you). Touch base with your bride via her maid of honor at least once before noon. Is there any last-minute task she needs you to do? If you plan to leave for the honeymoon the next morning, make sure your bag is packed before you put on your tux—you don't want to be late for the airport because your Hawaiian shirt is missing.

Suit Up

Confirm with your best man that all the guys know where they need to be and when. (If anyone is flying in at the last minute, call the airline and check on the status of the flight.) About an hour before you need to be at the ceremony or photo session, get suited up. (Tip: Pack a second shirt—particularly if it's summer—since ceremonies have been known to make guys sweat.) Do a fashion check on all your guys; you'll be held responsible if one shows up with brown instead of black shoes.

Make Nice

This is your chance to earn extra credit with your bride. Remember when we told you on page 42 that you need to get her a gift? Well, it's still true. And here's a great opportunity to present it in a romantic fashion that will make her swoon: write a note that tells her how much you love her and how you can't wait to have her as your wife, and attach it to her gift. Arrange for one of your men to make the delivery.

If faced with the proverbial cold feet, don't worry—warm toes are within reach. The diagnosis: Nervousness doesn't mean you're making the wrong choice. That frosty feeling is probably part performance anxiety because you want everything to go smoothly (you are about to declare your love in public), part excitement because you've been looking forward to the party, and, of course, part jumpiness because taking the plunge is enough to make anyone panic. All these emotions are creating one big knot in your gut.

The cure: Simply distract yourself. Think back to the first time she made you laugh. Let the priceless memory keep you smiling, not shaking, all the way to the altar. Keep the mood light by carrying on continuous bull sessions with your groomsmen. Practice your vows. Recite your toast. Don't think you're alone in your nervousness—she's probably experiencing it too. And don't forget to hug your mom. She always knows how to calm you down. Whatever you do, don't tell your least-likely-to-ever-marry friend about your nerves—he'll only make you feel weirder.

RECEIVING LINE

Mother of the Bride · Father of the Bride · Bride · Groom · Mother of the Groom · Father of the Groom

MARRIED? THERE'S MORE

Your duties won't stop once you're husband and wife. Instead you'll take on the new role of happy hosts. Whether or not you want a receiving line is up to you, but if you're down for the post-ceremony meet and greet, read on to find out what they're all about. And even if you're not wild about formal pictures, you'll want at least a couple shots of you and your new wife(!). After you've shaken the last hand, keep that grin going and say cheese. See below for tips on getting through both the receiving line and the photo session.

THE RECEIVING LINE

What: No matter how you organize the receiving line, its purpose is always the same: to give you the opportunity to greet guests, shake hands, thank them for coming, and encourage them to enjoy the party. Flanked by your bride and your parents (and maybe your wedding party), you can handle this in a couple of different ways.

When: The most common time (it's the one you see in movies) is just after you make your exit, outside your ceremony site. As guests leave the sanctuary, they'll informally queue up to be thanked and greeted, and to tell you how wonderful the ceremony was. Afterward, you can sneak off to take photos or simply follow the last to leave over to the reception.

You can also hold a receiving line as part of your transition from the cocktail hour to the reception. Along with both sets of parents (guests usually greet first the groom's parents, then the bride's, then you, then your new wife), you stand at the entry to your reception space and welcome each guest to the party. This is a great idea if you have to run off and take pictures in between the ceremony and the reception, and the cocktail hour site is different from the reception locale.

Much less common but definitely not unheard of is to stand at the entry of your ceremony site and greet guests as they arrive. Though it's totally unconventional, couples who've greeted guests this way have found it to be very relaxing since it takes the pressure off immediately.

What you need to know: Don't worry about getting everyone's name. Any guest who doesn't know you will surely introduce him- or herself first. Be gracious and keep that line moving. If you find yourself in a heavy conversation, tell the talker you'll catch up at the reception. On the other hand, you might decide to skip a receiving line and make more informal rounds of the tables. A great time to do this is during the first course, but be sure your bride is with you. This option is not recommended for weddings with more than fifty people, though.

TAKING PORTRAITS

What: Even if the two of you have chosen to put an artistic spin on your wedding day, you'll still need a photographic bare minimum of the two of you alone, with the wedding party, and with each of your families—after all, Grandma needs something to frame on her wall.

When: Decide beforehand with your bride (and your photographer) how you want to handle it. Some couples decide to forgo tradition and take shots together pre-ceremony (it lets you get right to the party later). Your photographer will probably set up a romantic first meeting, but if you're dead set on not seeing your future wife until the ceremony, this is not for you. In that case, your best bet is to grab the key players for post-ceremony picture taking, which will delay your arrival at the cocktail hour but preserve that moment when you first see her coming down the aisle. And here's an option if you plan on taking a lot of posed pictures: pre-ceremony, you and your bride can each take plenty of separate shots, and then after the ceremony you can do the group shots with the two of you together.

What you need to know: Formal portraits can be time consuming, with photographers estimating an average of five minutes per photo. If you budget five photos, at five minutes each, plus five minutes to get everyone to the snap session, that's already half an hour. Add five minutes for each additional grouping you desire (just the guys, just the girls, you and your grandma, for example). Plan ahead by ordering champagne and light bites for the session—no one likes to pose for pictures on an empty stomach, especially while the guests are living it up at the cocktail hour.

RELISHING THE RECEPTION

HOW TO BE A GOOD HOST

Number-one rule for the reception: don't be elusive. Even though you'll probably get only a minute or two with each guest, some sort of contact with you makes well-wishers feel special. Pose for photos if people ask, or drag the photog over to get certain people in a picture. Send a round of shots over to select tables if you dare. Boogie down with different people as you crisscross the dance floor. Be gracious, and try the tips below to prevent awkward interactions.

Know Your Roots

If you haven't seen second-cousin Sam since you were eleven, then you probably can't even remember how he's related to you. Before the wedding, ask your parents for a quick review of your family and their friends. Remember, everyone will know you, so it's only common courtesy that you be able to address each of your parents' guests by name.

Mind Your Manners

This may be the first time you meet your fiancée's extended family, so be on your best behavior. Keep your language clean and avoid political rants and sarcastic remarks. We're not saying you should pretend to be someone else, just that no matter who you are you'll need to be the guy who gets along with everyone today. Plan on making plenty of introductions. Having names and lineage under your belt will prevent bloopers. If you do have a momentary memory lapse, gracefully try to get the person to reveal something that will give you a clue. Otherwise, keep the talk brief but pleasant and move on.

Make an Escape

Be prepared for uncomfortable moments by having three pieces of universal conversation you can pull out with any guest ("Isn't the band great?" "Are you enjoying yourself?" and "Did you find it here OK?"). When you can't take another minute of someone's dull chatter, cut it short—when he or she comes up for air, wrap it up by saying how nice it has been to talk but that you must check in on your bride. You can even make a pact with her to keep an eye out for one another in sticky situations—the couple who ditches together stays together.

Kiss the Bride

Don't let the crowd distract you from your girl. If you can't make rounds together, make sure to meet up now and then for some hand holding, hugs, or even high-fives. Your bride will be feeling just as anxious as you, now that everything is coming together—not necessarily as planned. Never forget that your two-person team needs to stand unified.

→→→ **DEALING WITH EMERGENCIES**

Even the best-laid wedding plans can go awry. Something is bound to come up and, when it does, chances are you'll be the point person—particularly if you don't have a wedding coordinator. If some reception glitch (like they're running low on champagne) comes to your attention, ask your best man or good friend to solve the problem without involving your bride. No need to stress her out. She can find out later, when she'll simply marvel at your fantastic coping skills.

TIME(LINE) TO PARTY

Once you've survived the ceremony (and an hour of smiling for the camera), it's time to hit the reception. You can take or leave certain traditions for the night, but here are some key events where you'll take center stage.

Your Entrance

Usually the DJ or the bandleader makes an introduction, and guests all stand and cheer as you arrive. Go with a simple "Introducing the new Mr. and Mrs. Doe," and walk in with your bridal party. Or opt for something more dramatic such as a bubble or fog machine, walking in to the tune of "Let's Get Ready to Rumble" or the Penn State fight song. Obviously, check with your fiancée first. She may prefer something simple and sweet.

The First Dance

After the grand entrance, most couples choose to transition straight into their first dance. This makes sense—all eyes are on you, so you probably shouldn't just cross the room and take your seats, right? Plus, even if you've got four left feet between the two of you, your guests want to see a few romantic twirls on the dance floor. Before you break into a cold sweat, consider dance lessons. A pro can help you get from the first step to the final dip flawlessly in two to six weeks, and the time you'll spend together is a great diversion from pre-wedding stress. So go ahead and enjoy the first dance. Just don't step on her gown, and don't hold her *too* close—this is no time for the lambada.

Spotlight Dances

The first dance isn't the only dance required of you for the night–there's a special song with your mom too. And it's always a good idea to take the mother of the bride out for a spin; you won't need to request a specific tune for this one–just take a moment when the sound suits you. Other dance cards to sign? The maid of honor (your bride will dance with your best man) and maybe your bride's siblings too.

Dinner Is Served, and the Best Man Speaks

Toasting typically begins as guests are seated for the first dinner course. Tradition states that the best man kicks things off with a toast to the bride and groom (turn your chair to face him). Then comes your response, which includes some words for your bride.

Toasting Time

The father of the bride traditionally ends the toasting, thanking all guests for coming. This may not be the end, however–close relatives and friends may be clamoring for the microphone. So after the father of the bride's toast, the MC can welcome anyone to speak: the bridesmaids, maid of honor, your parents, your grandparents. Just be sure everyone knows to keep it short and sweet. At the end, the best man or MC takes over

HOW TO OPEN CHAMPAGNE

Remove the foil from the cork.

Untwist the wire restraint securing the cork.

Angle the bottle away from everyone.

Gently untwist the cork.

Slowly ease the cork out of the bottle's neck.

Listen for the pop and pour.

and announces the start of the festivities. (Our complete guide to toasting follows on page 137.)

The Garter Toss

The "for the boys" version of the bouquet toss is all yours. Your bride is brought to the middle of the dance floor with a chair. The DJ or band strikes up a (somewhat) risqué tune, she raises her hem slightly, and you slide your hands on up there and remove her garter. With your back to the assembled gaggle of guys, you hold it like a rubber band and let it fly over your shoulder. Sometimes the lucky guy who catches it will keep

Garter

the garter; other times he'll put it on the lucky gal who caught the bouquet. Your bride may want to take off her garter herself and slide it onto your leg. Then toss as you wish. (Note that putting your head under your bride's skirt doesn't seem as appropriate as it once did—although it's hard to imagine that it ever seemed appropriate.)

Cutting the Cake

Another must-do. Even couples not serving a traditional wedding cake will usually have the baker or caterer whip up something from which they can snip a slice. Plan ahead when you'll do it so your bandleader or DJ can get everyone's attention (and so the two of you won't be taking a bathroom break or otherwise unavailable when he makes the announcement). If you've got a multiple-tier cake, be sure to make your cut to the bottom tier (and avoid a collapsing cake crisis). Use a fork to feed a bite to your bride (she'll do the same for you). Don't smash cake into her face. The cake-cutting tradition symbolizes your promise to nurture each other, so don't put a bad spin on it.

The Grand Finale

Couples are always finding creative ways to exit with a bang, whether escaping for their honeymoons or just joining guests at the after-party. Pick a great last song, then transition into a "time to go" tune that will usher the two of you (and your guests) out the door—anything from a bagpiper to Marvin Gaye's "Let's Get It On." An elaborate send-off is always a favorite, plus it makes for great photos. Run through sparklers, a shower of rose petals, or even a fleet of zooming paper airplanes. Once you're out, hop into a fun getaway mobile: a boat, fire truck, pedicab, or tricked-out limo will all make for an unforgettable exit.

The After-Party

On one hand you want to get to your hotel suite, but on the other hand you want to keep this celebration in full swing. Go ahead and continue the fun with friends. Your bride is in no hurry to remove her gown—she wants to play the princess card for as long as possible. The honeymoon suite will wait. Here are some ideas for post-wedding fiestas:

- Rent out the bar or a private room in the hotel where everybody is staying.
- Go bowling—your bride will look adorable in her gown and those funny shoes.
- Keep with your newfound love of public speaking and head to a karaoke bar.
- Hit the city's hottest dance club. The tux will make your running man look better.
- Feeling lucky? Bring your gang to a casino and have your wife roll the dice.
- Kick off your shoes and build a bonfire at the beach. Toss in your little black book to get the flames going.

THE VIRTUAL GROOM: Hit the Web to confirm your honeymoon reservations. Take advantage of the flight status notification tool offered by many airlines. If there's a change in your itinerary—a flight is delayed, cancelled, or the gate's been changed—they'll leave you a voice mail or a text message immediately.

→ → → **SAVORING THE BRIDAL SUITE**

If you don't leave for your honeymoon immediately from the reception (which can make for a pretty hectic exit), you'll most likely spend your first night as husband and wife in a hotel suite. You both may be so tired that the thought of romance seems like a distant memory. But you should be prepared, in case you're both feeling romantic. Here are some ideas for how to impress your bride with your thoughtfulness.

- The obvious: scatter rose petals on the bed, put champagne on ice, and set out chocolate-covered strawberries.
- Place a framed photo of the two of you by the bedside.
- Set up a portable stereo with a selection of her favorite CDs.
- Arrange lit candles throughout the room.
- Have a gift waiting for her: a gorgeous piece of lingerie.

TIPS ON TOASTING

Exchanging vows at the ceremony and giving a toast afterward are a large part of the wedding. Feeling jittery? Relax. You're not addressing Congress or accepting an Oscar—it's just your friends and family sitting before you, patiently awaiting a few genuine words of warmth, wisdom, and wit. However, wedding-day nervousness can tie the tongue of the most eloquent, seasoned speaker.

You've got at least two chances to wow them with your words: the rehearsal dinner and the reception. Take a deep breath and loosen up. You will be a perfect host. The recipe for success: choose words wisely, keep the nervous giggles and snorts to a minimum, and speak from the heart. If that fails, follow our foolproof guide. We've included everything from tips that guarantee an enthralling and entertaining speech to a step-by-step toast maker that'll have guests gushing about what a great speaker you are.

GIVING THE PERFECT TOASTS

The Rehearsal Dinner

Just because you'd rather be enjoying the filet mignon at the rehearsal dinner does not mean you'll get away without saying anything. This is the small stage—the warm-up for the big day. You won't need to say anything earth shattering (just your thank-yous). Follow the tips below to bring on the compliments.

Words to live by: Tell your fiancée that you love her and how excited you are about the wedding. It's essential to reinforce how lucky you feel to be marrying her. You cannot say this enough, and she will never get sick of hearing it. Since it's usually the groom's and his folks' affair (and a chance for your mother to feel like she's doing something useful), give a shout out to your parents for organizing the dinner and all the love and support they give you. Get sentimental if that's your style, and give mom a kiss and dad a hug.

Don't forget: Throw your brother or sister a bone (but do not inflict nouggies). Get campy if your family has a good sense of humor but avoid prop routines. Thank attendants and out-of-town guests for traveling long distances to join in the celebration. You don't want to get bogged down in details, but it's OK to throw out a few fond memories of the time Uncle Ray taught you how to cook a succulent steak and crazy Cousin Melvin snuck you into a Redskins game. It will make everyone feel included.

The Wedding

Giving the reception toast comes with a little more pressure because so many more people will be listening, but let's focus on the positive. You get to gush to your circle about how happy and grateful you are. The tone of your toast should change slightly from the rehearsal-dinner ditty. There are no set rules, but the groom typically speaks after the toasts given by the best man and bride's father, either before or during the meal. You can also speak just before the cake-cutting ceremony so it doesn't seem like yours is one of a string of toasts. Besides, you'll already have everyone's attention at that point.

Words to live by: Don't go into this thinking you can fly by the seat of your pants. Create an outline beforehand. Don't apologize for being a bad speaker or admit that giving this toast is the last thing you want to be doing. This will not help you gain sympathy—only a kick on the shin from your wife in her pointy shoes. As in the rehearsal-dinner speech, you must start out by complimenting your bride and pledging your undying love for her. This is not a recommendation. Ignore this and everyone in the room will think one of three things: you're selfish, your toast is a failure, or you're nervous. None is good.

Don't forget: The evening's sponsors—your in-laws. You may be a funny guy and your new dad might be a real Rodney Dangerfield type, but emotions will be running high and an attempt at humor can go south very quickly. Refrain from sarcasm, irony, and references to biological activities. Let the thank-yous fly—certainly for the terrific party, but most of all for their precious daughter. Make nice. It's good insurance. Once the new fam is content, give a quick nod to your mom and dad. In closing, raise your glass to all the wedding guests and give your wife a loving kiss.

TOASTING GUIDELINES

Perfecting your words boils down to five easy steps.

Step 1: Have a Plan

There's a lot of ice to break, but you've undoubtedly got your pick of engaging anecdotes. Start light and amusing, but steer clear of puns and slapstick. "I just flew in from Miami—man, are my arms tired!" is a poor opener. This is your wedding toast, not a Borscht Belt comedy routine. Begin with a story about your bride that makes you grin (but avoid anything dirty)—remember, whether your language is clever or corny, sappy or sharp, you must never be foul or uncouth. And whatever you do, don't forget to thank the folks who pulled the wedding together (and paid for it!). Find your toasting formula and stick to it (a good one is quote + anecdote + thanks = you're done!).

Step 2: Choose Your Words

Keep your language simple—you don't need to show off your vocabulary, especially if it's not so expansive. This is not the time to test out new adjectives like "malevolent." Work hard to banish words such as "like," "um," and "you know" from your patter. It's OK to use these place holders when speaking with friends but not when making a suave speech.

Step 3: Do a Practice Run

Walking up to the stage with a stack of index cards looks rehearsed. You need to seem spontaneous but not too off the cuff, so you'll need to practice. Try writing down a list of key words and names you want to touch on, instead of every word of the toast. Stand in front of the bathroom mirror and do some test runs. It'll sound different every time but you're not going for verbatim—you just want to make sure you hit the important points. It would really suck to thank your college track coach for making you team captain and forget to say a word about your beautiful bride.

Step 4: Worry

No, seriously. Use nervousness to your advantage. Strategize like Tiger Woods. You think he doesn't get a little knock-kneed before the U.S. Open? Some healthy anxiety will give you much-needed momentum and make the moment extra exciting. Before you begin, take full, deep breaths from your lower lungs—real belly inhales. This little breathing exercise tricks your body into relaxation.

Step 5: Pace Yourself

Finally, speak slowly but say it quickly. Two or three minutes is sufficient for a toast, especially if your bride wants to speak too. Yes, people want to hear a good speech, but not a twenty-minute discourse on your love. Get in and get out fast, and keep your guests happy.

SPEECH SHORTCUTS

Stumped on what exactly to say? You're not alone. Whether you're gregarious or mellow there's inspiration at every turn. Think globally and spice up your speech with traditional quotes from around the world.

> *Try to reason about love and you will lose your reason.*
> –French proverb
> *When the husband drinks to the wife, all would be well;*
> *when the wife drinks to the husband, all is.*
> –English proverb
> *Marriage has teeth, and him bit very hot.*
> –Jamaican proverb
> *Let's drink to love, which is nothing unless it's divided by two.*
> –Irish toast
> *Love is like a baby; it needs to be treated gently.*
> –Congolese proverb
> *Love and eggs are best when they are fresh.*
> –Russian proverb

Another option? Turn to literary passages.

> *Insomuch as love grows in you, so beauty grows. For love is the beauty of the soul.*
> –St. Augustine
> *We never live so intensely as when we love strongly. We never realize ourselves so vividly as when we are in the full glow of love for others.*
> –Walter Rauschenbusch
> *To love someone deeply gives you strength. Being loved by someone deeply gives you courage.*
> –Lao-tzu

Love does not consist in gazing at each other, but in looking outward together in the same direction.

–Antoine de Saint-Exupéry

One word

Frees us of all the weight and pain of life:

That word is love.

–Sophocles

Night and day you are the one,

Only you beneath the moon and under the sun.

–Cole Porter

At the touch of love everyone becomes a poet.

–Plato

Love is a fire that feeds our life.

–Pablo Neruda

Love is friendship set to music.

–Anonymous

International flavor and literary connections not working for you? Break the rules and think outside the champagne flute. Create a list of the top ten reasons you love her, or the reasons you are meant to be together. Create a "this is your life" slide show or videotape. Maybe recite a parody of a well-known song or poem that celebrates your love. Perhaps list her wonderful attributes using the letters of her name. Read from old love letters, or prepare a list of all the things you never thought you would like but now do because of her (like eating sushi and jogging in the park). No matter what road you choose, always consult with your bride–even if you're not toasting together.

EPILOGUE:

I f you've made it this far, congratulations! The engagement period is an amazing time for you and your bride. If you recognize that, then you've got the goods to really start your new life together right. Get ready to take the plunge and look forward to the next phase in your life: marriage.

The ten best things about being married:

1. No more wedding planning (just home decorating).

2. You get to call her "my wife." Not bad, huh?

3. Joint bank accounts.

4. Growing old together.

5. Sex.

6. Being your silly self around her all the time.

7. The security of having a best friend in good times and not so good times.

8. Someone to come home to every night (and a meal, whether home cooked or take-out).

9. What was "hers" and "yours" is now "ours."

10. Do you really need another reason?

WEB GUIDE FOR THE GROOM

Here's a cheat sheet to the best of TheKnot.com for grooms, plus a few extra resources to fill in the blanks.

Chapter 1: Getting Started

www.theknot.com/budget	Create the perfect interactive budget that will recalculate projected costs once you start spending the dough.
www.theknot.com/guestlistmanager	Keep track of who's invited, whether they're on the A or B list, and their RSVP status.
www.theknot.com/webpage	An easy way to create your own Web page to keep guests (and your groomsmen) informed of wedding-day details. The best part? It's free!
www.bridalassn.com; www.weddingconsultant.com	Looking for outside help? Check out the Association of Bridal Consultants, or the Association of Certified Wedding Consultants.
www.wedsafe.com	Weddings disasters begone! Consider signing up for wedding insurance for the big day.
www.weddingtracker.com	Sign up at this site for your own personalized domain name ($70 for 1 year) with the capacity to upload 200 pictures to your wedding Web page.

Chapter 2: Bride Management

www.theknot.com/askcarley	Don't understand what your bride's talking about? Here's your one-stop etiquette shop.
www.theknot.com/grooms	From great gift ideas for your bride to do-it-yourself boutonnieres, this is your central wedding-advice station.
www.gia.edu	Diamonds are a girl's best friend (after you, of course). Learn about the four c's from the Gemological Institute of America.

Chapter 3: A Guy's Guide to Wedding Planning

www.theknot.com/local	Find great bands, photographers, and limo companies in your city.
www.theknot.com/talk	Chat with other brides and grooms in your area to get reliable recommendations.
www.theknot.com/createagift	This is an etiquette-friendly way to get cash for your wedding.
www.theknot.com/honeymoon	Get the details on honeymoon hot spots and pick up some travel tips for your getaway.
www.theknot.com/honeymoonquiz	Discover your perfect post-wedding paradise.
www.theknot.com/shop	Find essential wedding keepsakes, favors, and ceremony items.

| www.astanet.com | Take the guesswork out of honeymoon planning by using the perfect travel agent. Get references from the American Society of Travel Agents. |
| www.chowhound.com | Get recommendations for the best restaurants for your honeymoon locale. |

Chapter 4: The Wedding Players

www.theknot.com/groomsmen	What's expected of your main men? Find out here.
www.theknot.com/groomsmengifts	Pay your guys back for all the planning they did—for your bachelor party.
www.groups.yahoo.com	Set up a formal listserv for your groomsmen to keep them on top of wedding responsibilities.

Chapter 5: Wedding Wear

www.theknot.com/tuxedo	Browse through tuxedo styles to find your perfect wedding wear and locate stores in your area.
www.afterhours.com; www.tuxedos4u.com; www.menswearhouse.com	These formalwear companies have stores all across the country to make coordinating tuxes easier on your long-distance groomsmen.
www.ebay.com	Bid on antique cuff links, studs, and more.

Chapter 6: The Ceremony

www.theknot.com/ceremony	Find inspiration for your vows and ceremony readings.
www.theknot.com/local	Be prepared: read up on your city's marriage license requirements.
www.celebrantusa.org	Ordain your best friend. This is a nonprofit educational institution that trains people to become wedding officiants.

Chapter 7: The Finish Line

www.theknot.com/music	Preview songs for your first dance and your mother-son dance.
www.theknot.com/toasts	Stumped for words? Try our fail-safe tips on toasting.
www.bartlelby.com	Get inspired by the greats. This site contains more than 11,000 searchable quotes.
www.instantweddingtoasts.com	At a total loss for your toast? Have your speech customized by professional writers—for a small fee.
www.champagne.fr	Find the perfect champagne to suit the occasion.
www.thenest.com/checklist	Stay on track with your post-wedding to-do list.

Note: Log on to www.theknot.com/groomsbook to get an up-to-date list of groom-friendly resources plus hot links to all sites on this list.